Biological Diversity and Conversation

Biological Diversity *and* Conversation

Dr. Ahmad Husain

Mohit Publications
New Delhi - 110002

First Published 2006

ISBN 81-7445-359-8

Published by :
MOHIT PUBLICATIONS
4675/21, Ansari Road, Darya Ganj
New Delhi - 110002
Phones : 23255141, 23284136

PRINTED IN INDIA

Published by Smt. Sangeeta Goel for Mohit Publications, New Delhi-110002,

Printed at
R.S. Offset Printers Delhi–110053

Preface

At the world convention for biological diversity, the definition for biological diversity was recommended. Biological diversity means the variability among living organism from all sources including interalia, terrestrial marine and other aquatic ecosystems and the ecological complexes of which they are part. This includes diversity within species between species and of ecosystem. This book contains ten chapters. The first chapter of Biological Diversity explains Biological Diversity must be treated more seriously as a global resources to he indexed, used and above all preserved. The second chapter is of the forests in India. They defined a forest type as a unit of vegetation which possesses broad characteristics in physiognomy and structure sufficiently pronounced to permit its differentiation from other sub-units. Sixteen kinds of forests are being narrated in this chapter. Next chapter includes the wildlife in India Forest and wildlife in placed in the concurrent riot of the constitution of India. Impact of liberalisation an environment is also included in this book.

—Editor

Contents

	Preface	*v*
1.	Biologic l Diversity	1
2.	The Forests in Indi	21
3.	The Wild-Life in Indi	55
4.	St tu s of Biodiversity in Indi	63
5.	C s e Study Insect Diversity in High Altitude Forest	75
6.	Aqu tic Resources nd Fish Biodiversity	96
7.	C s e Study Insect Diversity in A Moist Deciduous Forest	113
8.	The Convention on Biologic l Diversity	130
9.	Environment l Difficulties in Developing Countries	166
10.	Imp ct of Liber liz tion on Environment	197
	Index	*221*

1

Biological Diversity

Life on this earth has constantly evolved for last four billion years to form the present spectacular richness of living world. The fossil records indicate that, on average, life has steadily increased in diversity and complexity over time to produce the present richness. The current popular term for this richness and diversity of life is Biodiversity or Biological diversity. Biodiver-sity means the wealth of life forms found on earth, in the form of millions of different plants, animals and microorganisms, which are further diversified with vast potential of future creation of the biodiversity from the ocean of genomic diversity, at the effectively functional level within the living biomass, the genes they contain and the intricate systems they form.

At the world convention for biological diversity, the following definition for biological diversity was recommended (UNEP 1992): "Biological diversity means the variability among living organisms from all sources including, interalia, terrestrial, marine and other aquatic ecosystems and the ecological complexes of which they are part; this includes diversity within species, between species and of ecosystems". Though this definition was fully accepted and adopted until 1995 all over the world, the definition in its make, context, concept and conformity altered and deviated variously and variedly (Balaji and Rai, 1999; Bhattacharya, 2000 and

Khoshoo, 2000). These alienations infused confusion and fallacies both in its actual and basic concepts. Kour (2000) reported that 14 different definitions exist of diversity. Presently, biodiversity is defined as "the intrinsically-inbuilt plus the externally-imposed variability in and among living organisms existing in terrestrial, marine and other ecosystem at a specific period of time". The diversity includes the variability in the genes, genotypes, species, genera and families and ecosystems in a specific region at a specific time period. Inclusion of all the above given variables and addition of the interactions existent amongst these, renders the assessment of the overall biodiversity intricate. Therefore, the diversity of the above mentioned different components represented each at genetic-, species-, population- and ecosystem-levels needs to be assessed and evaluated individually at each single level at a specific period of time and thereafter may be considered on an overall and on general basis. For instance, biodiversity at the genetic level represents the diversity of genes, which make up the germplasm of the species population. To this diversity, adds the diversity existing amongst various species that constitute the community. This species-diversity enhances the borders of biodiversity as it includes the variability existing within and between species and the interactions rampant amongst them. This harmonious existence and stability potential plus the genotype-environment interactions encapsulate them in a balance and sensitive system-the ecosystem.

The diversity existing among the various ecosystems in a region constitutes the ecosystem diversity. Hence, the interlocked interactions, both negative and positive existing amongst these three major levels of biodiversity, *viz.*, the genetic, the species and the ecosystem, represent the general and total biodiversity of an area at a specific period of time. With the passage of time, the biodiversity changes due to the species-replacements, populations interactions and ecological succession. These changes are accentuated by the human-influence. Thus, the term biodiversity is therefore, used in the literature to cover both the number of different populations and species that exist and the complex interactions that occur among them. Biodiversity, therefore, is commonly considered at three different levels:

1. Within species (interaspecific) diversity; usually measured in terms of genetic differences between individuals or populations.
2. Species (interspecific) diversity; measured as a combination of number and evenness of abundance of species.
3. Community or ecosystem diversity; measured as the number of different species assemblages.

1. ***Genetic diversity :*** Genes are the biochemical packages passed on by parents that determine the physical and biochemical characteristics of their offsprings. Although, most of the genes are the same, subtle variations occure in some genes. The result of these variations may be obvious, such as size and color, or may be invisible, for example, susceptibility to diseases. Such genetic variability has made it possible to produce new breed of crops plants and domestic animals, and in the wild allowed species to adapt to changing conditions.

2. ***Species diversity*** : A group of organisms genetically so similar that they can interbreed and produce fertile offsprings is called a species. Horses and Zebras are different species. They are genetically similar and can interbreed but all offsprings are infertile. Species are usally recognisably different in appearance, allowing an observer to distinguish one from another, but sometimes the differences are extremely subtle. The species diversity is usually measured in terms of the total number of species within descrete geographical boundries.

3. ***Ecosystem diversity*** : The functional relationships within and among the communities and their environment are frequently complex, but they are the mechanisms of major ecological processes such as water cycle, soil formation, nutrient cycling and energy flow. These processes provide the sustenance required by living communities and

so a critical inter-dependence results. Two different phenomena are frequently referred under the heading of ecosystem diversity: (*a*) the variety of species within different ecosystems—more diverse ecosystems contains more species, (*b*) the variety of ecosystems found within a certain biogeographical or political boundry.

Biodiversity is, therefore, an expression of both numbers and difference and can be seen as a measure of complexity.

Biological diversity must be treated more seriously as a globel resource, to be indexed, used and above all, preserved. Three circumstances conspire to give this matter an unprecedented urgency include: (*a*) exploding human populations which is degrading the environment at an accelerating rate, especially in tropical countries, (*b*) science is discovering new uses for biological diversity in ways that can relieve both human sufferings and environmental destruction and, (*c*) much of the diversity is being irreversibly lost through extinction caused by the destruction of natural habitats.

Though nature and natural forces stabilise the biodiversity of an area, humans destabilise this by selective-exploitation, elimination, destruction of the species needed for use or not needed by them. Therefore, the biodiversity in an area, in a region, in a zone, in a country and in a continent is ever changing and is neither static, nor is nature controlled but is fully human-tailored. Hence, evaluation and assessment of biodivesity at species and at ecosystem levels becomes invalidated due to human invasion and influence. The biodiversity at the species level is also altered by selective retention and or cultivation of the species needed by humans and by the elimination of the species not of immediate use to humans. This alters the ecosystem biodiversity of an area as the species constitute the basic component of an ecosystem. Therefore, the biodiversity at the species-and at the ecosystem levels for an area is valid only at the time it is studied, evaluated and assessed, because humans constantly cause alteration in it.

THE EXTENT OF BIOLOGICAL DIVERSITY

Estimates of total number of species present on earth today range over more than an order of magnitude, from a low around 3 million to a high of 30 million or possibly much more. At the same time we have a little idea of the rate at which species currently becoming extinct. The systematic naming and recording of species begin relatively recently, with Linneaus' work in 1758 recognising some 9000 species. Recent studies indicate that about 1.4 million living species of organisms exist in this world. Approximately 750,000 are insects, 41,000 are vertebrates and 250,000 are plants. The

Table 1. Species known to exist (adapted from mcneel et. al., 1990).

Group	No. of described Species
Bacteria	4,760
Algae	26,900
Fungi	46,983
Mosses and Liverworts	17,000
Gymnosperms	750
Angiosperms	2,50,000
Protozoans	30,000
Sponges	5,000
Corals and Jellyfishes	9,000
Round worms and earthworms	24,000
Crustaceans	24,000
Insects	7,51,000
Other arthropods and minor invertebrates	1,32,000
Molluscs	50,000
Starfishes	6,100
Fishes	19,056
Amphibians	4,184
Reptiles	6,300
Birds	9,198
Mammals	4,170
Total	14,35,662

remainder consists of a complex array of invertebrates, fungi, algae and micro organisms. Many taxonomists agree that this picture is still very incomplete except in a few well-studied groups such as the vertebrates and flowering plants.

If insects, the most species rich of all major groups, are included, the absolute number is likely to exceed 5 million. Thus remarkably we do not know the exact number of species on the earth. According to May (2002) the total number of species that have been named and recorded emphasises the uncertanties caused by the synonyms. The IUCN survey estimates that around 13,000 new species are currently named each year, but current rates of resolving synonymies reduces this number to around 10,000 distinct new species added yearly to be known total.

Table 2 : Number of named, distinct species of eukaryotes.

Group	Hammond (1995)	May (1999)
Protozoa	40,000	40,000
Algae	40,000	40,000
Plants	2,70,000	2,70,000
Fungi	70,000	70,000
Animals	13,20,000	10,80,000
(i) Vertebrates	45,000	45,000
(ii) Nematodes	25,000	15,000
(iii) Molluscs	70,000	70,000
(iv) Arthropods	10,85,000	8,55,000
(v) Arachnids	75,000	75,000
(vi) Insects	9,50,000	7,20,000
(vii) Others	20,000	20,000
Others	95,000	95,000
Total	17,40,000	15,00,000

There is a wide variation on the amount of taxonomic efforts being carried out in identifying the unknown species in different groups. According to May (2002) roughly one third of all taxonomists working on vertebrates, another third working on the ten times more numerous plant species, and the remaining third on invertebrate animals, which outnumber vertebrate species by atleast a factor of 100.

According to May (1999), the current global total of distinct eukaryotic species that have been named and recorded is around 1.5 million. This is lower than Hammond's (1995) 1.74 million, but is consistent with Wilson's (1988) estimate of 1.4 million roughly 10 years ago. All such estimates are mainly dominated by total number of insects. The other factor is our ignorance of the ecological and evolutionary forces, which underpin these interesting but empirical species, size patterns.

Where Does Most Biological Diversity Occurs

Biological diversity occurs within all habitats, because genetic diversity has allowed life to adapt to the harshest of environments. However, species are not spread evenly over the earth and biological diversity is greater in some areas than in others. Some habitats, particularly tropical forests among terristrial systems, have a great number of species. Tropical forests cover only 7% of earth's land surface, yet they are estimated to contain at least 50% of all species. Equally important, they are being depleted faster than any other ecological zone. Tropical deforestation is by no means an even process. Some areas are being affected harder than others; some will survive longer than others. The outlook for the future seems all the more adverse, though its detailed dimensions are even less clear than those of the present. Tropical biotas seem to have been unduly prone to extinction. But the remanant forest refugia usually contained sufficient stock of surviving species. To recolonize suitable territories when moister conditions return. Within the foreseeable future, by co 3ntast, it seems all too possible that most tropical forests will be reduced to much less than one-tenth of their former expanse and their pockets of holdout species will be much less stocked with potential colonisers. A 13.7 Square Km. area of the La Selva Forest Reserve in Costa Rica contains almost 1,500 plant species, more than the total found in 243,500 Square Km of Great Britain, while Equador harbours more than 1300 bird species or almost twice as many as the USA, and Canada combined (Myers, 1988). Mittermeier (1988) and Mittermeier and Werner (1990) recognised that a very small number of countries situated mainly in the tropics possess a large fraction of the world's species diversity, and introduced the term of "Megadiversity Countries", which they suggested, merit special international attention. McNeel et. al., (1990) used country species lists of vertebrates, swallowtail butterflies and higher plants to identify 12 such megabiodiversity countries : Mexico, Colombia, Equador, Peru, Brazil, Zaire, Madagaskar, China, India, Malaysia, Indonesia, and Australia. Together these countries hold upto 70% of the world's species diversity in these groups. This approach is relatively simple in that it involves species inventory within a given geopolitical boundary. It also recognises that conservation action is managed at country level. There may be considerable overlap in species composition between different regions with high species numbers, particularly if they are situated close to one another geographically. For example, in terms of mammal species in megadiversity countries Equador with 271 species and Peru having 344 species, 208 species are common to both the countries.

Lanly (1982) discussed the rate of change in the tropical forests and his data show that of the 11.3 mha of mature forest land deforested annually, 5.1 mha are converted to secondary forest fallow. He estimated that the total area of this forest type is 409 mha and that almost 1 mha of secondary forest is created annually on unforested land through natural regeneration or human intervantation. Such large forest area cannot be dissmissed as irrilevent to the conservation of species diversity because they support an extensive biota and because under certain conditions, they are capable of supporting more complex biota than the mature system they replace.

Many explanations have been put forward to explain the latitudinal gradient in diversity, none is completely satisfactory but they are not mutually exclusive and some can be effectively combined. The catastrophe hypothesis argues that all stable environments encourage diversification in time and since the tropics have been stable for longer than temperate regions, which have suffered catastrophic changes in climate in the form of ice ages, one would expect greater diversity in lower latitudes. Regions that have suffered other sorts of catastrophes such as volcanic activity, have lower diversity and therefore provide good supporting evidence. The related evolutionary speed hypothesis similarly argues that because conditions are more favourable in the tropics, organisms develop faster and go through more generations per unit time. Biota in warmer climates will evolve at more rapid rate than those in cold climates because of the more constant favourable conditions throughout the year, and therefore, faster generation times. Since temperate and polar regions are also younger, because of recent glaciations, the result is greater diversity in tropics; whilist temperate regions are still filling up with species.

The energy input hypothesis argues that diversity is related to available solar energy at a given location. Since the tropics receive more solar energy than the poles, one would predict a diversity gradient. The productivity hypothesis predicts that diversity is dependent upon the realised annual evapo-transpiration (RAE), which is very high in tropical rain forest, but is very low in a hot desert, explaining the difference in the level of primary productivity in these two environments. The simplest explanation is the area hypothesis, which predicts that larger areas of uniform climate will support more species than similar but smaller areas. The basis of this idea is that larger areas provide more opportunity for isolation of populations and therefore speciation.

VALUE OF BIODIVERSITY

Humans have always relied on the natural world and, despite our technological development; this remains just as true today. Biological diversity existing on this planet has a great value. There is a multiplicity of ways of assessing value of biological resources. Economists, in particular, have tried various approaches but difficulty lies when applying a common formula to the variety of resources used by man. The value of forests in terms of logs, for example, would be measured in a different way from the value of forest for recreation or watershed protection. In the terms of Norton (1988) species can have value as commodities, and as ameneties and they can also have moral values.

A species has *commodity value* if it can be made into a product that can be brought and sold in the market place.

A species has *amenity value* if its existence improves our lives in some non-material ways *e.g.*, the joy we experience in sightseeing, bird watching and the walks we enjoy in the middle of a forest.

Species have values as a *moral* resource to humans, as a chance for humans to form, re-form and improve their own value systems (Norton, 1984).

Mc Neely *et al.*, 1990 have used three main approaches to determine the value of biological resources:

1. *Consumptive Value:* the value of natural products *e.g.,* firewood, fodder and game meat-these are consumed directly and do not pass through a market.
2. *Productive Value:* the value of products that are commercially harvested, such as game meat sold in market, timber, ivory and medicinal plants.
3. *Non-Consumptive Value:* indirect value of eco-system functions, such as watershed protection, photosynthesis, regulation of climate and soil production.

Than there are two more values added to biological resources:

1. *Option Value:* intangible values of keeping options open for the future.
2. *Existence Value*: value attached to the ethical feelings of existence. The concensus is that whatever methodology is used, valuation is only a

fundamental first step. It informs planners, resource managers and local people about how important biological diversity may be to national development objectives. It further demonstrates how important an area is for the biological resources it contains, it reveals common interests in various sectors, and it facilitates comparison of costs and benefits of different development proposals. The second step is to determine how these species and areas can be conserved.

LOSS OF BIOLOGICAL DIVERSITY

The extinction of species has always been a natural part of evaluation. The fossil records show that since life originated about four billion years ago the vast majority of species that have existed are now extinct. Extinct species out-number living ones by a factor of perhaps a thound to one. As reviewed in details by May (1999) and Spekoski (1992), the average life span of a species in the fossil record, from origination to extinction, is typically a few million years which is of the order of 106 to 107 years. There is however, much variation within and among groups.

Extinction is the complete disappearance of all individuals of a species without producing progeny. Two broad processes are believed to affect the dynamics of population, and casue extinction.

1. Deterministic Process or cause and effect relationship *e.g.,* glaciation or direct human interven-tations such as deforestation.
2. Stochastic Processes or chance or random events, which may act independently or influence variation in deterministic process.

The magnitude of effects of these processes depends on the size and degree of genetic connectedness of populations. Four types of stochastic processes can be distinguished:

1. *Demographic uncertainty* : this only a hazard for relatively small populations, which number tens or hundreds of individuals.

2. *Environmental uncertainty* : due to unpredictable changes in weather, food supply and disease and the populations of competitors, predators or parasites.
3. *Natural catastrophes* : foods, fires and draughts.
4. *Genetic uncertainty* : random changes in genetic makeup, to which several factors contribute.

Vulnerability of Species to Extinction

There is considerable evidence that the number of species in an isolated habitat will decrease over time. The crucial issues for conservationists is whether those species which are most at risk for extinction after habitat fragmentation can be predicted from a knowledge of their biology and ecology. According to Laurance (1991) at least nine ecological or life history traits have been proposed as factors determining animal species sensitivity to fragmentation these are:

1. ***Rarity:*** Abundance of species before fragmentation is a significant predictor of extinction. Newmark (1991) found that after fragmentation, rare under story birds occupied fewer forest fragments per species than common ones. This is related to the fact that fewer individuals of a rare species than common species are likely to occur in habitat fragmentation.
2. ***Dispersal ability:*** Animals capable of migrating between fragments or between main land areas and fragments are able to mitigate effects of small population size. Good disperses are therefore, less prone to extinction in fragmented habitats.
3. ***Degree of specialization:*** Ecological specialists often exploit resources which are patchily distributed in space and time, and therefore, tend to be rare. Specialists may also be vulnerable to successnational changes in fragments and to the collapse of evolved mutualism and food webs.
4. ***Niche location:*** Species adapted to, or able to tolerate, conditions at the interface between different

types of habitats may be less affected by fragmentation than others. *e.g.*, forest edge species may benefit from habitat fragmentation.

5. ***Population variability:*** Species with relatively stable populations are less vulnerable than species with pronounced population fluctuations, since they are less likely to decline below some critical threshold from which they may not be able to recover.
6. ***Trophic status:*** Animals at higher trophic levels are less abundant therefore, more prone to extinction because of rarity.
7. ***Adult survival rate:*** Species with naturally low survival rates may be more likely to become extinct, as proposed by Kar (1991) for terristrial birds on Boro Colorodo Island, Panama.
8. ***Longivity:*** Long-lived animals are less vulnerable to extinction than short-lived ones.
9. ***Intrinsic rate of population increase:*** Populations, which can expand rapidly, are more likely to recover after population decline than those, which cannot.

IUCN CATEGORIES OF SPECIES

The following categories of rare plants and animals have been recognised by the International Union for Conservation of Natural Resources (IUCN), mainly based on (*i*) present and past distribution, (*ii*) decline in number of populations in course of time, (*iii*) abundance and quality of natural habitats, and (*iv*) biology and potential values of the species. These are defined as follows for the purpose of conservation:

1. ***Endangered (E)***: This includes the species which is in danger of extinction and whose survival is unlikely if the casual factors continue operating. Included are the taxa whose numbers have been reduced to a critical level or whose habitats have been so drastically reduced that they are deemed to be in immediate danger of extinction.
2. ***Vulnerable***: This includes the taxa believed likely

to move into the endangered category in the near future if the casual factors continue operarting. Included are the taxa, of which most or all the populations are decreasing because of overexploitation, extensive destruction of habitat or other environmental disturbances; taxa with populations that have been seriously depleted and whose ultimate security is not yet assured; and taxa with populations that are still abundant but are under threat from serious adverse factors throughout their range.

3. ***Rare (R):*** It includes the taxa with small world populations that are not at present endangered or vulnerable, but are at risk. These taxas are usually localised within restricted geographil areas or habitats or are thinly scattered over a more extensive range.
4. ***Threatened (T):*** The term threatened is used in the conservation context for species, which are in one of the categories of endangered, vulnerable and rare. Some species are marked as threatened where it is known that they are endangered, vulnerable or rare, but there is not enough information to say which of these three categories is appropriate.
5. ***Out of Danger (O):*** It includes the taxa formerly included in one of the above categories, but which are now considered relatively secure because the effective conservation measures have been taken or the previous threats to their survival have been removed.
6. ***Intermediate (I)*:** This includes the taxa that are suspected of belonging to one of the first three categories, but for which insufficient information is currently available.

Concept of Keytone Species

Some biologists have used the term keytone species to identify certain species, which may be important in determining the ability of large numbers of others to persist in the community. Protecting keytone species is a priority for conservation efforts, because if a keytone species is lost, numerous others may disappear. Top predators are obvious keytone species, since these often control herbivore populations, but also be inconspicuous species. For example, Raven (1976) has argued that the extinction of each of tropical plant species potentially results in an additional loss of 10-30 insect species. This is because many tropical insects appear to be highly specialized in their feeding behavior, often only existing in one single plant species.

CAUSES OF EXTINCTION

The global loss of biological diversity has been described as a product of two phenomena:

1. Population levels have forced the transformation of relatively undisturbed areas into lands used for agriculture, and
2. Both industrial and agricultural pollutans have applied a new and narrowly uniform selective pressure on species.

The start of industrial revolution brought with it a whole new range of impacts and a new scale of human activity. The society largely took the view that nature was for humans to control and resources were there to be exploited. Chiras (1994) expresses this mind set as the frontier ethic that many societies, religious groups and nations espoused. The frontier ethic has three tenets:

1. There's always more and its all for us. In which the earth is viewed as an unlimited supplier of resources for human use.
2. Human are apart from nature and immune to natural laws. Originating from religious based philosophy in which humans view themselves as so special that they are somehow unreleated with the rest of the living world.
3. Human success derives from the control of nature. Since humans are apart from nature they are in

competition with it and must dominate and control it to be successful.

World's economic strategy and measurement of its success still embrace these ethics. With the rapid growth of the industrial economies the living standard of people has also developed with an increase in the per capita resource use. Thus, we are all, as an individual, using an increasing amount of the earth's resources to the extent that there is now global competition for them.

Population growth and technological changes have multiple, rather than simply additive impacts on biological diversity. However, from a conservationists point, the various agents responsible for decline in biodiversity are classified under four headings:

1. Over kill,
2. Habitat destruction and fragmentation,
3. Impact of introduced species,
4. Chains of extinction.

Dimond (1984) called these "the evil quarter". From an analysis of factors responsible for known and threatened extinctions of vertebrates, Jenkins (1992) has shown that introduced animals and direct habitat destruction are major contributors. 39% of species have become extinct through introductions and 36% through habitat loss. Hunting and deliberate exterminations contribute significantly (23%) of extinctions with known causes.

1. **Overkill:** Overkill results from hunting at a rate above maximum sustained yield. The most susceptable species are those with low intrinsic rate of increase, because of their limited ability to recover quickly. Hence, although usually having a high standing biomass when unharvested, they give a low maximum sustained yield, which is easily exceeded. They are even more vulnerable if valued either as food or as an easily marketable commodity. The harvesting of wild plants and animals is still a major human activity. As humans became more numerous and wide spread they started to kill species faster than those species could replace

themselves, either through reproduction or immigration from else where. Population will crash if we continue to remove natural resources at a greater rate than they can be replaced. Thus the vulnerability of species to overexploitation is partly predicted by their capacity to increase. Apart from the direct threat of overkill of a species, there are indirect consequences for the communities and ecosystems to which these species belong. All species play definite role within ecosystems. However, some species play a unique and important role in ecosystem function and their removal results in fundamental change in that system.

2. **Habitat destruction and fragmentation:** The most direct threat to biodiversity comes from destruction of the habitat on which it depends. Although habitats may be modified, degraded or mearely eliminated, it is more commonly fragmented. A large tract is converted piecemeal into another land use. This process is common throughout the world, as can be seen not only in India but also in many countries specially the developing countries. Loss of habitat by a given proportion does not increase the vulnerability of a species, not decreases the numbers of its members, but that same proportion, except in the special case of habitat being cleared from the edge inward. More commonly the modification produces a patchwork of pattern as it errodes the tract of habitat from inside and changes microclimate. At first the areas occupied by the new land use provides the continuous phase and the original habitat the discontinuous one. The vulnerability of species then increases disproportionately.

In developing countries, the patterns and causes of habitat destruction are linked to economic growth. In economically weak developing countries rapid population growth causes economic and political problems that require resources. These are provided at the expence of the environment, mainly through forest clearance. Ehrlich (1995) develops the argument that habitat destruction is linked to human enterprise, which in turn is directly correlated with energy usage. Therefore, if habitat destruction is a major cause of species extinction, both of these will increase as the human population grows. The annual loss of forest cover in some of the developing countries is given below:

3. **Impact of introduced species:** Species intentionally or unintentionally introduced by people have produced to exterminate native species by competing with them, preying upon them, or destroying their habitat. A review by Atkinson (1989) has demonstrated that 22 species and subspecies of reptiles and amphibians have disappeared worldwide due to alien animals. In New Zealand alone, 9 species of reptiles and amphibians and 23 bird species have become extinct since AD 1000 through introduction. The introduction of exotic species into some areas has had a devastating impact on the native biodiversity. Native species most vulnerable to the impact of exotic species introduction are those, which have evolved in isolation from high levels of competition and predation. The majority of recent extinct species inhabited small isolated oceanic island.

Table 3 : The average annual loss of forest cover (103 ha/year) in some of the developing countries.

Country	Current annual loss of forest cover
Brazil	2554
Cameroon	129
Columbia	581
Costa Rica	41
Ghana	117
Indonesia	1084
Laos	148
Madagascar	130
Mexico	508
Nigeria	121
Peru	217
Tanzania	323
Thailand	3[illegible]
Venezuela	503
Vietnam	135
Zaire	740

Some of these, such as the Dodo, were early targets for sailors for much needed protein, but many more smaller flightless birds, were victims of species introduced by man, accidently or deliberately. There are a number of characteristics of species that make them good invaders:

(i) Species with a high reproductive rate that can quickly build up a large population size under favourable conditions.

(ii) Generalists species with broad habitat requirements and diet that are likely to be able to find somewhere suitable to live and something suitable to eat.

(iii) Good dispersers that can travel across the new area and find suitable habitats.

Similarly there are a number of characteristics of places that may make it easier for introduced species to become established:

* Early successional areas or disturbed areas with empty niches tend to have resources that are unexploited and available for immigrating species with little or no competition.
* Remote islands with low taxonomic diversity are vulnerable because few species have been able to colonise and communities and food webs are often simple with potential empty niche space to be exploited.
* Remote islands with no predators and native prey providing an easily exploited food source.

4. **Chains of extinctions:** The extinction of one species may cause the demise of others, this is known as secondary extinctions. Diamond (1989) gave as example the extinction or near extinction of genus *Hibiscadelaphus* as a consequence of the extinction of several species of pollinators, the Hawaiian honeycreepers. Examples of predators and scavangers dying out after the species providing their food died out are also common.

WHY CONSERVE BIODIVERSITY

There are two good reasons for conserving biodiversity. The first is moral: it is right to do so. The second is practical: bilogical diversity supports human survival, notably through health, food and industry. The fundamental social, ethical, cultural and economic values of biological diversity have been recognised in most of the human disciplines, from religion to science. Given these multiple values it is not surprising that most cultures consider the importance of conservation. Despite this and in order to compete for the attention of the government decision makers throughout the world, policies regarding the protection of biological diversity must embrace economic values.

The concern for biological diversity is, however, a concern for man himself. All forms of life-human, animal and plants, are so closely interlinked that disturbance in one gives rise to imbalance in the others. If species of plants and animals become endangered they signify degradation in the environment, which may threaten man's own exixtance.

In India, the conservation ethic was imbibed in the sylvan surroundings of the *Ashrams* of our sages, which were the seats of learning in the country's ancient past. The love and regard for flora and fauna is a part of India's culture. A hymn of the Yajur Veda invokes universal peace with special mention of the " let there be peace of air, peace of earth, peace of waters, peace of plants and peace of trees". This reference to Vedic Poetry reveals how responsive the Indian sensibility was, in the earliest days, to the benidiction of nature and wild life. The lofty Upanishadic speculations about mans spiritual destiny were undertaken in the deep peace of forest retreats. The very name, *Aranyakas* or Forest Texts reveals this significant connection between India's spritual heritage and sylvan milieu.

2

The Forests in India

The word forest is derived from the Latin 'foris', which means 'out of doors'. A forest is a biological community dominated by trees and other woody vegetation as defined by the society of American foresters. Forest is a living system and not just a community. According to Spurr and Barnes (1964), forest ecology is concerned with forest as a biological community with the interrelationships between the various trees and other organisms constituting the community, and with the interrelationships between these organisms and the physical environment in which they exist. The forest consists of highly stratified (up to 5 strata) vertical structure and represents climax formations.

Forest shows a grate range in variation in their species composition, physiognomy, dominance, etc., due to differences in climate, edaphic and biotic factors in different areas. Thus, on the basis of these parameters, different types of forests have been identified.

Champion for the first time presented a classification of forest type of India, which was later modified by Champion and Seth. This classification recognises 16 forest groups arranged in 6 major forest type *viz.*, moist tropical forests, dry tropical forests, montane subtropical forests, mountain temperate forests, subalpine forests and alpine scrub. Each forest group was divided into subgroups. They identified a total of 221 ecologically stable vegetation types.

Table-1 : Forest type of India, their groups and sub-groups (after Champion and Seth, 1968).

Forest type and forest group	Forest sub-group
Forest type I: Moist Tropical Forests	
1. Tropical wet evergreen forests	
	(i) Southern tropical wet evergreen forest
	(ii) Northern tropical wet evergreen forest
2. Tropical semi-evergreen forests	(i) Southern tropical semi-evergreen forests
	(ii) Northern tropical semi-evergreen forests
3. Tropical moist deciduous forests	(i) Andamans moist deciduous forests
	(ii) South Indian moist deciduous forests
	(iii) Indian moist deciduous forests
4. Littoral and swamp forests	(*i*) Littoral forests
	(*ii*) Tidal swamp forests
	(*iii*) Tropical seasonal swap forests
	(*iv*) Tropical riparian fringing forests
Forest type II: Dry Tropical Forests	
5. Tropical dry deciduous forests	(*i*) Southern tropical dry deciduous forests
	(*ii*) Northern tropical dry deciduous forests
6. Tropical thorn forests	(*i*) Southern tropical thorn forests
	(*ii*) Northern tropical thorn forests
7. Tropical dry evergreen forests	
Forest type III: Montane Subtropical Forests	
8. Subtropical broad-leaved hill Forests	(*i*) Southern subtropical broad-leaved hill Forests
	(*ii*) Northern subtropical broad-leaved hill Forests
9. Subtropical dry evergreen forests	

They defined a forest type as a unit of vegetation which possesses broad characteristics in physiognomy and structure sufficiently pronounced to permit its differentiation from other sub units.

FOREST TYPES OF INDIA

1. Tropical Wet Evergreen Forests

These forests develop in the conditions of high temperatures associated with excessive rainfall (more than 250 cm) found in Western faces of Western Ghats, parts of Mysore, Bengal, Assam and Andaman Islands. The floristic composition of vegetation varies in different regions, however, *Dioterocarpus* is almost common in the forests of North India and *Hopea* in the South. Other important species are *Artocarpus*, *Dysoxylum* and *Mesua*. These forests exhibit the features of tropical rain forests and consist of evergreen trees with close canopy. These climatic climax forests are well stratified (4-5 strata) with highest species diversity. The species, which form the uppermost canopy of stratum, are usually more than 75-100 m high. The lower strata consist of comparatively small trees, shrubs, lianas, climbers, epiphytes, palms, canes and bamboos. The herbaceous vegetation on the ground is very low in diversity and density because the dense tree canopy does not allow sufficient light penetration for the development of floor vegetation, thus palms bamboos, ferns and other herbaceous species are usually shade tolerant.

2. Tropical Semi-evergreen Forests

These forests are distributed in parts of Assam, Kalinpong, Western Ghats, Orissa hills and Andamans where annual rainfall ranges between 200 and 250 cm. These forests show the recurrence of a relatively long dry period resulting into semi-evergreen forests. The dominants include deciduous species but evergreens predominate. The general canopy is typically less dense than the true evergreen. These forests also show luxuriant growth of giant trees with shrubs, orchids, ferns and herbaceous ground vegetation. In Assam, species of *Phoebe* and *Amoora* are common, whereas in Western Ghats *Diospyros, Bombax* and *Aporosa* are common. Other species in northern forests are *Dipterocarpus*, *Artocarpus*, *Michelia*, *Terminalia*, *Albizzia*, *Mangifera*, *Shorea*, *Mallouts* and *Xylia*. Climbers are not conspicuous.

3. Tropical Moist Deciduous Forests

These forests occur in the areas with annual rainfall between 100 and 200 cm spread over the year with a short dry period and are distributed on the eastern side of Western Ghats, Chhota Nagpur, parts of Orissa, eastern Madhya Pradesh, Gangetic Plains, some Himalayan foot-hills, Assam Valley and in Andamans. The dominant species are mainly deciduous but subdominant and lower canopy trees are largely evergreen. The canopy is rarely dense and even but over 25 metres high. The deciduous species shed their leaves in March-April period. The trees of lower storey are usually not tall (not exceeding 30-40m). These forests are dominated by *Tectona grandis (*teak), *Dalbergia latifolia, Terminalia* and *Grewia* in the south, and by *Shorea robusta* (sal), *Albizzia*, *Terminalia* and *Mallotus* in the north. In Andamans, *Pterocarpus*, *Lagerstroemia* and *Terminalia* are common dominants. Grasses include *Andropogon*, *Cymbopogon, Heteropogon* and *Apluda* as common genera.

4. Littoral and Swamp Forests

These forests occur in wet and marshy coastal areas. The tidal forests occur in river deltas, for example, in the deltas of river Ganga on the east coast. The littoral species are mainly evergreen, of varying density and height, but always associated with wetness. *Casuarina equisetifolia* is the most characteristic species on sandy beaches and dunes. The mangrove vegetation which occur in coastal areas consists mainly of *Rizopora, sonneratia, Heritiera, Avicennia, Acanthus,* etc. The swap region in the Bengal delta is known as Sundarban which is named after Sundari tree (*Heritiera fomes).* The mangrove in this swamp includes the species like *Phoenix, Pandanus, Nipa* and *Heritiera.* The Indian mangroves have only 14 species, which are mostly and extensively distributed in the Sundarban.

5. Tropical Dry Deciduous Forests

These forests prevail over the areas with an annual rainfall ranging between 75 and 125 cm. and with about 6 month long dry season. Most of the trees remain leafless during dry season. These forests occupy about 40% of the toral forest area of the country, with a distribution throughout the Peninsula (except Western Ghats), Madhya Pradesh, Gujarat, Maharashtra, Karnataka, Andhra Pradesh, Madras, Punjab, Bihar, Uttar Pradesh and Orissa. The forests are stratified in 2-3 layers. The top canopy is rather light and rarely over 25 metres high, usually 8-20 metre. The undergrowth is well developed in these forests. The dominant tree in the Northern forests is sal (*Shorea robusta)* and in the southern forests teak (*Tectona grandis*) is most conspicuous. Other species include *Anogeissus, Terminalia, Madhuca, Aegle, Dendrocalamus* (a bamboo) and *Bauhinia vahlii* (a climber) in the northern forests, whereas the southern forests in addition to teak have *Terminalia, Pterospermum, Acacia, Dalbergia, Diospyros, Boswellia,* etc., with *Dendrocalamus* (a bamboo), *Bauhinia vahlii* (a climber), *Phoenix sylvestris* (a palm) and parasites like *Loranthus, Viscum, Vanda and Cuscuta.*

6. Tropical Thorn Forests

These forests occur in the areas with high temperatures and very low (20-70 cm) rainfall characterising a dry and hot season which is much prolonged. These areas include parts of southern Punjab, western Rajasthan, parts of Upper Gangetic Plain, Gujarat, Madhya Pradesh, Maharashtra and Tamil Nadu. The plants are deciduous with thorny features. Canopy is more or less broken with a height less than 10 metre. Plants remain leafless for most part of the year and give an expression of scrub vegetation. The plants include acacias (*Acacia nilotica, A. senegal, A. catech, A. arabica, A. leucophloea,* etc.) as dominants. Other plants include the species of *Madhuca, Bombax, Euphorbia, Randia, Salvadora, Calotropis, Adhatoda, Zizyphus,* etc. Shrubs are more frequent than the trees. The herbaceous vegetation develops extensively during rainy season. These forests are regarded as degraded tropical dry deciduous forests.

7. Tropical Dry Evergreen Forests

These forests occur in the coastal areas of Tamil Nadu and Karnataka where annual rainfall does not exceed 100 cm. The dominant trees are hard leaved evergreen with some deciduous emergents, often dense, but usually up to 20 metres in height. The grasses and forbs constitute the herbaceous vegetation. The bamboos are absent. Important trees include *Manilkara, Terminalia, Sterculia, Ixora,* etc.

8. Subtropical Broad-leaved Hill Forests

These forests are classified as montane forests of India with all the temperate (high altitude) forests. These occur on outer slopes of the Himalaya, Bengal, Assam and the South Indian hills. The trees are broad-leaved, largely evergreen. The common species in the northern forests are *Quercus, Alnus, Cedrela, Castanopsis, Populus,* etc., whereas the southern forests are mainly composed of *Eugenia, Terminalia, Murraya, Ficus, Pterocarpus,* etc.

9. Subtropical Pine Forests

These forests occur in the Himalaya between the altitudes of 1000 and 2000 m. the pine forests occur as open stands of *Pinus roxburghii* in the Western Himalaya and *Pinus khasya* in the Eastern Himalaya. The associates of *Pinus* include *Quercus* (oaks) and *Myrica.* Common shrubs include *Berberis, Rubus, Rhus,* etc. These forests are mostly burnt by fire during summers.

10. Subtropical Dry Evergreen Forests

These forests are distributed at lower elevations in the Himalaya where annual rainfall ranges between 40 and 80 cm. Due to low rainfall, these forest are xerophytic, but the evergreen nature of the vegetation is due to low temperature. The forests are open with thorny and small-leaved evergreen species such as *Acacia modesta* and *Olea cupisdata.*

11. Montane Wet Temparate Forests

These include the high rainfall regions of the Eastern Himalaya and some parts of South India (Nilgiris). These forests are broad-leaved and evergreen and occur in the mountainous areas. Conifers are absent in these forests. The trees are of medium size and have a dense growth forming the closed canopy. Epiphytes and climbers are abundant. These forests in the south are called 'sholas' in which the common species are *Eurya japonica, michelia nilgirica, Hopea parviflora, and Ternstroemia.* The forests in the Eastern Himalaya are distributed between the altitudes of 1800 and 2900 m with the common plants of *Quercus, Acer, Alnus, Machilus, Mahonia, Rhododendron,* etc. These forests also have a good undergrowth.

12. Himalayan Moist Temperate Forests

These forests are found between the altitudes of 1500 and 3000 m in the Eastern and Western Himalayan ranges where the annual rainfall ranges between 100 and 250 cm. These are the evergreen forests mainly composed of oaks and conifers. The trees form a very high canopy sometimes reaching up to 45m. The conifers are needle-leaved, whereas the oaks and other angiosperms are broad-leaved. The common species in the Western Himalaya include *Quercus leucotrichophora, Q. semecar-pifolia, Q. floribunda, Q. dilatata* (all oaks), *Abies pindrow* (fir), *Pinus wallichiana* (blue pine), *Cedrus deodara* (Deodar or cedarwood), *Picea smithiana* (spruce), while the common species on the Eastern Himalayan sector include *Q. lineata, Q. pachyphy-lla, Abies densa, Picea spinuloa, Tsuga dumosa,* etc. *Taxus baccata and Rhododendron arboreum* are distributed in both the regions of the Himalaya. The undergrowth is thin in these forests.

13. Himalayan Dry Temperate Forests

A narrow dry belt extending from Himalayan parts of Uttar Pradesh through Himachal Pradesh and Punjab to Kashmir at elevations similar to the moist temperate forests of the Himalaya (1500 to 3000 m) and with a rain fall less than 100 cm is occupied by Himalayan dry temperate forests. The vegetation is almost evergreen and is dominated by oaks and conifers. The coniferous forests are open with sparse xerophytic undergrowth. Conifer forests/patches are more common than oaks. The trees attain a heigt upto 50 m. The common genera include *Cedrus, Abies, Pinus (wallichiana) Quercus, Rhododendron, Juniperus,* etc. The scrubby undergrowth consists chiefly of *Artemesia, Alnus, Daphe.,* etc. These forests also occur in the Eastern Himalaya where the slopes are drier with low rainfall. The common species in this part of the Himalaya are *Quercus, Picea spinulosa* and *Betula.*

14. Subalpine Forests

These forests are stunted deciduous or evergreen forests usually in close formation, with or without conifers, occurring at elevations from 3000 m to tree line in the Himalaya. The common species are *Picea smithiana, Abies (A. spectabilis* in the west and *A. densa* in the east), *Betula utilis, Rhododendron campanulatum,* etc. with common shrubs like *Contoneaster, Rosa, Berberis, Lonicera, Ephedra,* etc.

15. Moist Alpine Scrub

This vegetation occurs in the Himalayas above the timber-line and extends up to about 4500 m. The altitude of the timberline is at about 3600 m or above in the Western Himalaya, but in the Eastern Himalaya, this limit of trees is usually much higher to that in the Western Himalaya. The vegetation is mostly dense and consists of evergreen dwarf species for *Rhododendron, Juniperus* and *Betula utilis.*

16. Dry Alpine Scrub

This scrub occurs in stony habitats such as limestone rocks where the rainfall is very low (below 35 cm). The vegetation consists of xerophytic scrub in open formation. These include mainly the species *Juniperus (Juniperus communis* and *J. wallichiana* in the Western Himalaya and *Juniperus recurva* in the Eastern Himalaya), and *Betula utilis.* Total percentage of area covered by different forest types in India is given in Table-2.

Table-2: Percentage of area covered by different forest types in India

Forest type	% Area covered
1. Tropical wet Evergreen Forests	8.0
2. Tropical semi-evergreen Forests	4.1
3. Tropical Moist Deciduous Forests	37.0
4. Littoral and Swap Forests	0.6
5. Tropical Dry Deciduous Forests	28.6
6. Tropical Thorn Forests	2.6
7. Tropical Dry Evergreen Forests	0.2
8. Subtropical Broad-leaved Hill Forests	0.4
9. Subtropical Pine Forests	6.6
10. Subtropical Dry Evergreen Forests	2.5
11. Montane Wet Temperate Forests	3.6
12. Himalayan Moist Temperate Forests	3.4
13. Himalayan Dry Temperate Forests	—
1 4. Subalpine Forests and Alpine Scrubs	2.9

(source: Forest Survey of India)

CAUSES OF FOREST DEGRADATION

Increased urbanisation, industrialisation and mining has caused indiscriminate felling of trees and denudation of forests. The practice of logging down the trees for human use has been growing with the passing of centuries. Colonists used logs for firewood and making huts. Humans used the logs and other forest produce for various purposes. The problem of forest degradation is highly alarming in the Asian countries. Important causes of forest degradation are as follows:

1. Forest Fires

Forest fire is one of the mos important ecological factors in the terrestrial environment. It has affected a substantial portion of the forests of the world.

(i) **Kinds of Fires:** On the basis of the causes, the forest fires are of following two types:

(a) **Intentional Fires**: These are the fires, which are set intentionally. Sometimes miscreants set fire to the forest with an intention to damage the forest wealth. In Himalayan area, villagers set fire to the forest floor so as to induce a good growth of grass in the following season. This is an effect of over-population of cattle in this area. Controlled fires are also set by the Forest Department in some cases, but such fires hardly produce any harmful effect on the environment.

(b) **Unintentional Fires**: Tourists and poachers may cause these fires mainly, who may leave burning cigarette butts, matches, campfires etc., in the forest. Lightning also causes these.

On the basis of damage to the forest, the fires are of following three types:

(a) **Surface Fires**: These are mostly man-caused (intentional and unintentional) and are set to regenerate the growth of grasses and forbs in the grasslands. Surface fires sweep over the ground surface rapidly and their flames burn litter, living herbs and shrubs. Such types of fires also burn tree bases. Young plants such as those of pines may succumb to surface fires.

(b) **Ground Fires**: Fires sweeping the forest surface may generate ground fires, which burn in thick accumulation of organic matter. These fires are flameless and subterranean and almost all plants rooted in the burning material are burnt leaving the woody species with thick root barks.

(c) **Crown Fires or Wild Fires**: These fires are most destructive, killing all the vegetation from the ground upward. In the forests, these fires travel from one crown to another. Conifers are badly destructed by crown fires. Burried seeds and subterranean organs in the moist ground escape these fires.

(ii) **Effects of Fires**: Fire affects the vegetation directly or indirectly in various ways.

(a) **Direct Effects**: Surface fires and crown fires kill the vegetation of all types or injure them severely, whereas

the ground fires burn the undergrowth of the forest and some of the underground parts of the plants. Direct effects of fires include the burning of biomass, release of carbon dioxide and nitrogen gases and ash in the atmosphere and deposit of nutrients.

(b) **Indirect Effects**: Some of the effects of burning of forests are indirect. Fire causes removal of competition for surviving species which causes the abundant growth of the fire-resistant species at the cost of fire-susceptible species. The injuries or scars left on the stems of woody plants serve as sites for the entry of parasitic fungi and insects. Changes in the environmental factors such as the increase in light at the ground surface and soil nutrients, increase in soil organic matter and decrease in rainfall interception are also caused by forest fires. The fire also affects adaptations for some plant species. The fires in the forest also affect wildlife population and their habitats.

There are a number of plant species, which develop adaptations to the fire. Certain species of pines, oaks and shrubs develop thick bark or fire resistant seeds or fruits. Apart from the harmful effects of fires, it is useful in the management of vegetation. Fire induces regeneration and reproduction in some plant species such as of herbs in the grassland. Thinning of the ground surface also helps in sprouting and more growth of plants. Nutrition of the ground is also increased. Fire also eliminates the diseases and insect outbreaks.

2. Tree Felling

Tree felling was started for the domestic use and for the manufacture of agricultural implements and for the develop-mental activities such as for the supply of railway sleepers.

Wood smugglers in different parts of the country do the illegal felling. Villagers also remove illegally some of the forest produce in the form of fuel-wood or grass. Most villagers enjoy certain rights for collection of dry stems, barks, leaves, etc., from the neighbouring forest for their energy needs. However, dry twigs, leaves etc. from an average forest is seldom enough to supply the fuelwood needs of a village having about 40-50 families. The villagers are forced in such circumstances to extract more fuelwood from the forest, than is allowed under the rules.

Contractors sometimes cut down more trees than that is allowed. This practice was common during 1950s and 1960s. People used to enter the forests illegally and remove one or two trees. Some nomadic tribes in the Western Himalaya also do illegal felling of trees. They live int he forests and cut down the forest illegally. They earn their livelihood by selling milk to the nearby towns and village. The cumulative effect of these activities resulted in the forest degradation. However, with the abolition of the contractor system in most areas and introduction of very strict laws against illicit felling, this activity has been checked. But poachers and timber-wood smugglers in different parts of our country, which needs immediate attention and control through strict legislation and watch, are still doing the illegal felling. India alone is losing more than 1.5 million hectare or forest cover each year and according to Tiwari (1982) 22 million hectare of forests was destroyed during the three decades of 1950 to 1980.

3. Overgrazing

Overgrazing by cattle is one of the greatest factors in the degradation of pasturelands particularly in the Himalayan areas. Over the years, with the increase in cattle population, there has been a rapid degradation of the forest environment. In J & K, after 1970 the cattle population nearly doubled. 20% of the total cattle population of the country is in the Himalayan region, which has about 18 percent of the forest area of the country.

The cattle population is maintained for the following reasons:

(i) **Milk and Agricultural Uses**: Cows, goats and buffaloes are reared for their milk in different

villages. Some villages also depend upon Gujars or nomadic/seminomadic tribes for their milk requirement. Bullocks are used for ploughing the field.

(ii) **Manure**: Animal dung has a prominent place in hill agriculture where chemical manures are not in much use. Each farmer likes to keep about 10 animals per hectare of cultivation in the hilly areas. Many farmers also keep one or two stall-fed buffaloes, but stall-feeding of cows is rare. Usually, animals kept exclusively for this reason are allowed to graze on the pastures during the day and they are kept in enclosures during the night.

(iii) **Wool**: Some nomadic and semi-nomadic tribes in the hills and foot-hill zones rear goats, sheep and yaks for their hair, which is used to make woollen garments, blankets, carpets etc.

Ecological effects of over-grazing are as follows:

1. Over-gazing causes repeated grazing of grasses and forbs in the pasturelands, which affects their regeneration and growth.
2. Most of the species by repeated grazing develop into prostrate plants, which affects their normal growth and tolerance.
3. The carrying capacity of the pastures is not followed in overgrazing practice. When the number of cattle exceeds the carrying capacity of a pasture, these develop into degraded lands.
4. The plant species susceptible to repeated grazing are eliminated from the pasture, only the resistant species remain there. This affects the normal community status of such over grazed pastures.
5. Due to repeated movement of cattle in the same pasture, gullies are formed in their tracks which accelerate the soil erosion and land degradation
6. Cattle hooves also damage Young regeneration, seedlings and saplings of trees and shrubs.

4. MINING FOR ROAD CONSTRUCTION AND DEVELOPMENT PROJECTS

Mining is a biotic factor in which man is exploiting the resources of nature, especially the minerals. This activity is done for various purposes such as mineral extraction, road construction and major hydroelectric projects. These activities have reduced the mineral resource itself and at the same time have caused considerable adverse changes in the ecosystem. The extraction of minerals and materials requires removal of vegetal cover; soil mantle and excavating overlying rock masses (overburden), which commonly exceed the volume of material extracted. Some of the important minerals, which are extracted by mining, include limestone, dolomite, phosphorite, gypsum, graphite and magnesite.

Surface or open cast mining causes a considerable loss to vegetation and soil cover particularly in the Himalayan areas. Mining affects the distribution of plant species, reduces the vegetation cover and habitat, and causes the loss of soil cover and increases the soil erosion. This activity sometimes results into the instability of slopes in the hilly areas, landslides and silting-up of rivers. The abandoned mines are invaded by exotic species such as *Lantana camara, Euphorbia royleana, Eupatorium* species, etc. These lands ultimately get converted into waste-lands or highly degraded lands. Mining activity also affects the survival of native species such as orchids and some medicinal plants.

5. SHIFTING CULTIVATION (JHUM)

Shifting cultivation is a practice, which prevails throughout the world, particularly in the hills inhabited by tribals. In this practice, the cultivator does not use a particular piece of land year after year. A patch of land is selected, all the trees, herbs and shrubs are cut down at or near the ground level there, which are left to dry in the sun and then are set on fire. The cleared and burnt areas are then taken up for cultivation. Seeds are sown in the ground. This cultivation practice is carried out by human labour without ploughing the land or using animal labour.

Shifting cultivation is perhaps the most primitive form of cultivation. Over 2.6 million people belonging to tribes who live in the interior hilly area practice shifting cultivation in India. About 1.35 million acres of land is under this form of cultivation in India in Assam, Arunachal Pradesh, Andhra Pradesh, Meghalaya, Mizoram, Nagaland, Manipur, Tripura, Bihar, Orissa, Madhya Pradesh, Karnataka and Kerala. It is called Lo or Jhum in Mizoram and Assam and by other names in other parts of India.

Main crops raised include grain crops and also cash crops. Among the food grains, coarse varieties of rice is the principal crop, others are maize, millet, jowar etc. Vegetables include pumpkins, cucumber, melons etc. Cotton is also raised as a cash crop. One important feature of such areas is that the land under shifting cultivation does not get any replenishment of nutrients in the form of manure. Thus, yield from these areas starts diminishing from the second year onwards. The cultivators then move to a fresh patch of land. The cultivator usually does not return to the same land again.

The major forest types in which shifting cultivation is prac-tised in the Eastern Himalaya are tropical wet evergreen forest, tropical semi-evergreen forest, tropical moist deciduous forest, subtropical broad-leaved forest, subtropical pine forest, montane wet temperate forest and Himalayan moist temperate forest.

The environmental problems caused by shifting cultivation include:

1. Clearing and burning of vegetation reduces the forest cover to the loss of timber worth lakhs of rupees and and loss of other forest produce.
2. Tribals working in the interior forest areas draw much forest resources.
3. Damage to the vegetation cover leads to soil erosion, silting up of rivers, reservoirs, depletion of soil nutrients, floods, etc.
4. The Jhum cultivators accidently may set fire to the adjoining forest, which may affect the vegetation and its regeneration.

5. The abandoned cultivated areas remain fallow land for 10-15 years, which means a great loss as productive land is kept useless.
6. The rare or sparsely distributed plant species are destructed by the practice. Such species belong to genera *Michelia, Tetracentron, Betula, Taxus, Acer, Illicium,* etc.

6. TOURISM

Tourists are of different types based on their purpose such as pilgrims who visit a number of shrines and religious places, tourists who visit seasonal resorts, and the mountaineers and adventure sports-persons who visit the Himalayan and other hilly areas. The major environmental problems caused by tourism are as follows:

1. Health and sanitation problems are caused by tourism during the peak influx of tourists. Thc maintenance of eatables and drinking commodities becomes a tidy job and sometimes make these commodities unhygienic.
2. Tourism activity also causes a pressure on the forests. Due to large number of tourists, the grasslands and forests are destructed by horse riding and by fires, which are caused accidently. The horse owner makes a pressure on the forests for the fodder requirements of their horses during the season of tourism or pilgrimage.
3. This activity is also causing the pollution problems in the tourist areas. The mountaineers leave behind much garbage in the high altitude areas, which is a matter of concern these days.

7. NATURAL CAUSES OF FOREST AND LAND DEGRADATION

Besides the biotic causes, natural processes such as earthquakes, glaciers, mountain streams etc., too are creating environmental problems related to forest and land degradation. These processes are as follows:

Earthquakes: Earthquakes are also responsible for land degradation. This activity is highly destructive in the Himalayan and other hilly areas. Some of the important earthquakes, which took place in, the Himalaya and other parts of the country, are as follows:

(a) Kashmir earthquake (May, 1885)
(b) Assam earthquake (June, 1897)
(c) Assam earthquake(August, 1950)
(d) Kisnnaur earthquake(January, 1975)
(e) Dharchula earthquake (1980)
(f) Uttarkashi earthquake (October, 1991)
(g) Chamoli land slides and earthquakes
(h) Latur earthquake
(i) Bhuj, Kutch earthquake in Gujrat, 2001.

Earthquakes cause severe damage to land and forest in addition to the human life and animals.

Glaciers: A glacier may be defined as naturally moving body of large dimension, made up of crystalline ice formed on the earth's surface as a result of accumulation of snow.

Glaciers are a major source of erosion in the snow bound areas. They form U-shaped valleys, hanging valleys, crevices, cirques, glacial scars etc., by erosion and lateral, medial, englacial or ground moraines, drumlins etc. by transportation and deposition. Majority of the glaciers in the Himalaya occur in the main Himalayan range though some are found on off shoot ranges such as Pir Panjal and Dhauladhar ranges. Glaciers or rivers of snow after accumulation begins to slide slowly down the hill slopes under the effect of gravity.

The Sarbal glacier in the eastern Kashmir descends to 3700 m while the Gangotri glacier descends to 4000 m, Khumbu glacier form Mount Everest terminates at 4900 m and the Kanchenjunga glacier descends to an altitude of about 4200 m.

Receding glaciers leave behind unconsolidated debris, which may become the source material for landslides etc. In

Gangotri area of Garhwal Himalaya, heaps of recent morainic material can be seen in the temple area. Such features are also seen in the Everest and Pindari glacier areas.

Glaciers also cause erosion leading to the formation of very steep sides or the slope failures. As the sun rises, the level of the melt water stream goes up leading to flash floods during mid-day. This phenomenon is very common in the glaciers of Kashmir and Himachal Pradesh.

Snow avalanches: Snow avalanches account for the heavy movement of earth's contemporary mass. Each year, thousands of avalanches occur in the Himalaya, that individually involve masses between 100-10,000 tons and vertical descents between 100 to over 1500 m (Negi, 1982). Snow avalanche is simply the failure of snow-covered slopes. Avalanches are of various types on the basis of their movement.

Avalanches cause heavy damage to the landform conditions in addition to loss of property and agricultural area. They may lead to the formation of gullies, particularly along weak zones. Avalanches are a constant threat to forested land. They damage large chunks of forests. In most cases, the trees are broken at about breast height. Young trees and saplings are the most susceptible to avalanches as they have least resistance to the rushing mass of snow.

Stream erosion: More than 25 per cent of the geographical area of India falls in the Ganga drainage system, of this about 40 percent lies in the Himalaya. The erosion caused by river systems depends on the volume of water and its rate of flow.

Following three activities are responsible for the degradation of the land :

(a) **Erosion**: It is the most prominent activity of rivers particularly in the areas with a gradient. Erosion may lead to deepening of the river valley and other effects.

(b) **Transportation**: Rivers generally transport rock fragments, soil particles and salts in the dissolved form.

(c) **Deposition**: It begins under the conditions when the speed of the water decreases, under changes of temperature and pressure conditions, or when an obstruction occurs in the course of the river.

The load of the Himalayan streams and rivers consists of huge boulders and rock fragments. During flash floods, this material is deposited on agricultural fields, forest lands etc.

FOREST CONSERVATION

A Forest is an important renewable natural resource. Trees dominate the forest ecosystem, whose species diversity varies in different parts of the country and in different parts of the world. They play an important role in enhancing the quality of environment by influencing the life supporting system. The chief product that forests supply is wood, and other forest produce of minor importance are called minor forest products. The total forest area in our country is estimated at about 22% of the total area on the basis of remote sensing data (Forest Survey of India). Wood and minor forest products are the direct forest resources, whereas the indirect forest resources are the maintenance and improvement in the quality of soil, air by the forests.

The term 'forestry' stands for the theory and practice of constitution and management of forests and utilisation of their products. It also stands for the scientific management of forests. Forests need to be conserved and managed against their depleting cover. Forests are managed to obtain a sustained yield, which is obviously possible through sustained growth. Following considerations are important in the conservation and management of forests:

(i) A forest should have in correct proportion the trees of different ages and classes so that continuous removal of exploitable produce would not affect the future yield.

(ii) Each tree crop should have normal growth increments.

(iii) Unrestricted felling should be prevented.

For all planning in the conservation and management of forests, sound ecological knowledge is desirable that should include knowledge about climatic conditions, composition of community, successional trend, life cycle of important tree species, methods of control of undesirable trees and promoting growth of high yielding tree species.

Following methods are employed in the conservation and management of forests:

SOCIAL FORESTRY

Social forestry is simply defined as the forestry of the people, by the people and for the people. Social forestry means the management and protection of forests and afforestation of barren lands, with a purpose of helping in the environment, social and rural development, as against the traditional practice of securing revenue. The National Commission on Agriculture (1952) has classified social forestry into three broad classes *viz.*, urban forestry, rural forestry and farm forestry.

Social Forestry Practices: Following are the main practices included social forestry:

(a) Raising wind breaks on dry farm lands.
(b) Planting shelterbelts.
(c) Planting along roadsides intensively.
(d) Planting in the village common lands and wastelands.
(e) Planting along railway lines and canal banks.
(f) Planting small wood lots on the farm if it is large.
(g) Planting of garden near villages and along highways for recreation and rest.
(h) Planting foreshore areas of irrigation tanks.
(i) Planting of saline and calcareous soils unsuitable for agriculture.
(j) Recla mation of waterlogged areas or areas susceptible to inundations by planting trees.
(k) Planting of river and stream banks and trailing the rivers.

(l) Reclamation of highly eroded lands and controlling erosion.
(m) Raising of trees on soil conservation bunds.
(n) Planting of trees in urban area-environmental planting.
(o) Raising of irrigated plantation of teak and mulberry.
(p) Afforestation of command areas of irrigation projects.

Types of Social Forestry: The types of social forestry are as follows:

(a) **Farm Forestry**: This type of social forestry includes raising of wind breaks, shelter belts, farm wood lots, raising trees in village common lands etc. Windbreaks and shelterbelts are planted in the dry land agricultural areas. The higher speed of wind causes rapid evaporation of water. To control the effect of high velocity winds, the plantations are raised in the form of rows, which are called **shelterbelts**. These belts consist of rows of trees and shrubs, planted along the field borders at right angle to the prevailing high velocity winds. The belts are 3 to 5 rows of trees and with a conical cross section, that is, towards the windward side shrubs and bushes are planted close to each other, the second row will have medium sized trees and the third row tall trees, and then in the declining order. The common examples of plants in such belts are *Agave*, Falsa etc., in the first row, *Sesbania*, kubabul, etc., in the second row and third row with *Eucalyptus, Casurarina,* Acacias, etc. The shelterbelts reduce the wind velocity over the crops and also reduce the evaporation losses. The increase in dew formation in these belts is suitable for the good growth of some crops like sorghum. The belts also control the soil loss from the crop and deposition into the crop area. The planted trees also yield fruit, fodder, fibre, fuelwood and small timber.

The windbreaks are the rows of trees planted along field margins in the perpendicular direction to the most high velocity winds. Roughly seven per cent of the total area should be planted for effective protection. The windbreaks are raised by planting two close rows of fast growing deciduous and one parallel row of slow growing of longer living evergreen species (Tamarind). Other trees suitable for wind breaks are *Casuarina, Melia, Tamarix, Eugenia, Eucalyptus, Artocarpus, Grevillea,* etc. *Anacardium, Acacia, Casuarina, Agave,* etc., are suitable for coastal areas. Shrubs and grasses are also used in these breaks.

Wood lots and afforestations are raised on lands unsuitable for cultivation. Every village must have at least 10 per cent of its cultivated area relegated for this purpose. These wood lots will be the property of the whole village and the benefits should be utilised for the betterment of the village.

***(b)* Extension Forestry**: This also includes agro-forestry practice. In extension forestry raising tree crops on canal banks, railway lines and road sides, under high tension electric lines, irrigated plantations of forest trees, afforestation of foreshore areas of tanks and reservoirs, reclaiming lands unsuitable for agriculture with tree crops (agro-forestry) are done.

Afforestation of canal banks is an important practice in social forestry because with the development of irrigation and power projects, these banks are also increasing and are creating new sites for plantations. These are poor in fertility and need to be protected from erosion, which starts with rills and slowly gullies are formed and these create breaches in the canal. Tree growth protects the banks and also prevents evaporation of water in the canal. Canal bank plantations also serve as shelterbelts to many fields adjoining the canals. Economic and shade providing species are preferred in the canal bank plantations. These may yield fuelwood, pulpwood, fodder, fibre and timber. Bamboo and teak if raised in suitable well-drained soils will prove of high economic value. Bamboo can be harvested every three to four years. The other species include *Eugenia, Dalbergia, Mangifera, Terminalia, Tamarindus, Azadirachta, Eucalyptus,* etc.

Afforestation of railway line sides and under high-tension lines is done to make these areas green, which could reduce the noise pollution, caused by trains and also the heat, making the journey comfortable. These plantations also check the erosion along these lines. The species selected for such planting should be from the local areas as they can withstand the climatic conditions prevailing there. The species planted along railway tracks include *Agave, Sacharum,* teak, *Eugenia, Acacia,* etc.

Under high-tension electric lines the species, which are, short and do not interfere with the power lines should be selected to utilise such lands. Lemon grass, baib grass, *Vinca rosea* (a medicinal plant) and *Eucalyptus citriodora* (maintained as a bush) are the favourable species.

Afforestation of roadsides is done to maintain the ecological balance, to provide tree shade to the travellers, to obtain forest produce, to reduce the noise pollution, to decrease the soil erosion and for aesthetic value. The species suitable for such plantations are shisham, *Terminalia, Albizzia, Delonix, Cassia, Erythrina,* etc.

Afforestation of foreshore areas of irrigation projects and ponds in dry farming areas is another type of extension forestry. In the areas of irrigation projects the top soil is removed and the rocks get exposed. Such areas should be planted by hardy species such as *Eucalyptus, Acacia,* neem, *Albizzia,* teak, mango, etc.

For uncultivable and wastelands, reclamation is done to revegetate them. In bare areas, the planting is done in pits. In eroded areas trenches are made and gully plugging is also done. Species of *Cassia, Albizzia* and *Vitex* are suitable species. The practice of agro-forestry is also done in the areas where the crop could be grown between the rows of planted trees.

***(c)* Urban Forestry**: This includes the plantations of tees in urban areas as a forest or amenity planting to prevent and minimise pollution. Urban areas are affected by smoke, noise and dust whose adverse effect cannot be easily estimated. Sometimes roads and paths have narrow margins; therefore, tree planting should be done wherever conditions are favourable and suitable. Tall narrow crowned trees are selected for such situations. In some urban areas planting is done in parks or green belts. Species suitable for such plantings include *Cassia, Delonix, Ficus,* Mango, *Eugenia, Jacranda,* etc.

The amenity planting is done in the areas of public buildings, schools, colleges, hospitals, offices, monumental and historical gardens, crematoriums, cemetaries, industries and home gardens.

1. Restrained Felling

The concept of sustained yield in forestry denotes to management of forests in such a way that a modest timber crop may be harvested indefinitely, year after year, without being depleted. In such a case the annual decrements should be counter balanced by annual increments. Maximum limit of annual felling should be fixed and the annual growth should be increased through different silvicultural practices.

2. Selective and Block Cutting

Block cutting method is suitable for the forest having almost even-aged trees of a fewer number of species. In this method trees are harvested not at random but in blocks. For example, from 10 acre of such forestland 1-acre block may be harvested each year for 10 successive years. If each harvested block is receded successfully, 10 age classes would be available after this period, for the blocks 1 to 10 consisting of 1 to 10 years of age respectively. After the 10 year period 1 acre of 10-year-old stem may again be harvested each year. In block harvesting method, the ecological, aesthetic and recreational uses are not maintained.

The selective cutting involves the cutting of some of the selected trees from a mixed forest or from a patch having trees of different age classes. Dense patches are selected first to mark the well grown trees for harvesting. This practice is done for the whole forest without clearing a particular portion or block. This practice is carried out on year-to-year basis.

3. Reforestation

The forests harvested by block or selective cutting methods are reforested. The bare areas are subjected to planting or reforestation. Sometimes, the seeds from the trees left after cutting become dispersed, but this may or may not be uniform in distribution for raising the new crop. Therefore, artificial seeding is required for adequate management of the forests.

FORESTRY AND ECO-DEVELOPMENT IN RURAL AREAS

Eco-development stands for the proper development of an area without affecting its ecology adversely. Thus, in eco-development the development and ecological balance are carried simultaneously. The resources are used in a sustained manner and their exploitation is done with a limit so that they can sustain or are sustained by some measures such as afforestation.

Forestry plantations have been helpful in sustaining the development and economy of rural areas. The common practices include various social forestry plantations, which can be applied successfully in the rural areas. These mainly include the farm forestry and extension forestry including agro-forestry. In farm forestry shelterbelts, farm wood lots and tree planting on common village lands are practised. In extension forestry the plantations are made along canals, railways lines, roads, under high tension electric lines, irrigated plantation of forest trees, afforestation of foreshore areas of reservoirs, land reclamation and agro forestry are practised.

Different types of trees are selected for various areas suitable for plantation. The trees are selected according to the availability of space, climate and the purpose. Important plants selected for such forestry plantations include *Agave, Grewia, Sesbania, Eucalyptus, Casuarina, Cassia, Acacia, Albizzia, Dalbergia,* cashew nut, mango, banana, *Artocarpus,* neem, Bamboss, *Tamarindus, Tamarix, Moringa, Pongamia, Delonix, Jacaranda, Eugenia, Grevillea, Vitex, Saccharum.*

Cenchrus, Eulaliopsis, Terminalia, Bassia, Erythrina, Bougainvillea, Ipomoea, Ficus, etc.

The species selected are in most of the cases economic or multipurpose. The economic species may be yielding fruits, fibres, fodder, fuelwood, timber, or the species may be simply shade providing (especially along roads and canals). In some of the plantings deep-rooted plants are required particularly in the devegetated areas.

The forestry practices have proved to be a boon for the village economy as well as for maintaining the quality of the environment. Thus, it has a big role in the rural development in the following ways :

1 It provides a better environment.
2 The pollution is minimised.
3 It provides the basic needs of rural people for fuel-wood, small timber, manure leaf, fodder for cattle, fibre, minor forest produce such as gums, tannins, dyes, etc.
4 It provides raw materials for industries such as wood, wool, packing cases, slate frames, sisal fibre, tamarind extract, oil seeds, pulping and hutting material.
5 It provides shelter for insectivorous birds in the farms.
6 Shelter and wind breaks protect crops from wind.
7 Soil moisture in conserved.
8 Soil erosion is prevented.
9 The land unsuitable for cultivation is fully utilised.
10 Employment opportunities in rural areas are generated.
11 Noise pollution is reduced.
12 Recreational sites and opportunities are created for boosting rural economy.
13 The pressure on natural forests is reduced.
14 Rainfall is improved by Improved precipitation.
15 The villages achieve self-sufficiency by social forestry.

ETHNOBOTANICAL STUDIES

Man has been using the plant wealth for various uses since time immemorial. The early man discovered the uses of plants and new plant resources of economic importance were found out later with the development of human civilization. The cultivation of plants was a great evolutionary accomplishment that relieved some of the members of a tribe from food gathering and hunting duties and enabled them to devote time and thought to inventing, discovering and developing other facets of civilised life. In this highly industrialised world, modern man's life still depends fundamentally on agriculture. The three basic necessities of life, food, shelter and clothing, and other essentials are still derived mainly from the vegetable kingdom. Ethnobotany deals with the study, cultivation and uses of various plants and their products of economic importance which are essential for living and for the betterment of the life. The history deals with the uses of various food crops, timber and wood, and medicinal plants.

India is rich in the economic plants. Such plants may be wild, or may be cultivated. Some of the economic plants have been introduced into this sub-continent from other continents. These include food crops, fruits, vegetables and other types of plants.

IMPORTANT ECONOMIC PLANTS OF INDIA

Important economic plants of India are as follows:

1. **Cereal Crops:** All cereals are members of the grass family (Poaceae) that are grown for their edible starchy seeds. These constitute the principal food crops of India. Cereals were among the first plants to be domesticated. These crops have wide adaptability and thus are easy to cultivate in different climatic and soil conditions. The term millet is applied to a variety of small seeds. The principal cereals include wheat (*Triticum aestivum),* rice *(Oryza sativa*) and maize (*Zea mays*). The important millets are ragi (*Eleusine corocana*), foxtail millet (*Setaria italica*), barnyard millet (*Echinochloa frumentacea*), bulrush millet (*Pennisetum

americanum, syn. *P. typhoides*), etc. Barley (*Hordeum vulgare*) is also nother cereal of importance. Oats (*Avena species*) are less important. Similarly sorghum (*Sorghum vulgare*) is also important millet.

2. **Fibre yielding plants:** In India, fibres are obtained from different parts of different species. These crops are also grown in different regions of the country. The fibres are classified on the basis of nature and structure into following categories:

Vegetable fibres (excluding wood fibres) are often grouped into three types according to their botanical origin: (*a*) soft, stem or bast fibres, (*b*) hard, leaf or structural fibres, and (*c*) surface fibres. Most of the fibres belong to the bast fibre category. These include flax *(Linum usitatissimum),* hemp (*Cannabis sativa),* jute *(Corchours capsularis & C. orlitorius),* sunn hemp *(Crotalaria juncea),* etc. Jute has the strong fibre.

Structural fibres include manila hemp *(Musa textilis)* as the strongest one. Coconut fibre *(Coir)* is an example of hard fibre (also called structural fibre).

Surface fibres include cotton, which is obtained from the surface of seeds, Predominant species cultivated in India include *Gossypium hirsutum* (50% area), *G. arboreum* (29%), and *G. herbaceum* (21% area). *G. barbadense* has negligible area of cultivation.

Fibres are also classified according to their use. These groups are called textile fibres (cotton), brush fibres (palms), rough weaving fibres (palms, bamboss, grasses etc.), filling fibres (*Semul* or *Bombax ceiba),* natural fibres (bark) and paper making fibres (wood, textile fibres, grasses and sedges).

3. **Sugars, starches and cellulose products :** Different types of carbohydrates are also obtained from some plants. Sugars are obtained from sugarcane *(Saccharum officinarum)* stem, sugarbeet, sorghum *(Sorghum vulgare)* sugar palm *(Arenga pinnata),* toddy palm *(Caryota urens),* wild date palm*(phoenix sylvestris)* etc. These are obtained from stems or roots. Cellulose products are used in paper industry.

4. **Legumes:** Legumes (seeds or pulses and green pods as vegetables) are important food crops. Pulses are important source of proteins. Important legumes include lentil *(Lens esculenta)*, pea *(Pisum sativum)*, chick pea *(Cicer arietinum)*, soyabean *(Glycine max)*, pigeon pea *(Cajanus cajan)*, horse bean *(Vicia faba)*, groundnut *Arachis hypogea)*, common beans *Phaseolus* species), lablab beab *(Lablab purpureus)*, green gram *(Vigna radiata)*, black gram *(vigna mungo)*, etc.

5. **Vegetable oils and fats:** Vegetable oils are classified into non-drying oils, semi-drying oils and drying oils. Important vegetable oil yielding plants include groundnut (*Arachis hypogea)*, mustards *(Brassica* species), coconut *(Cocos nucifera)*, oil palm *(Elaeis guineensis)*, common olive *(Olea europea)*, castor *(Ricinus communis)*, cottonseed (*Gossypium* species), sesame *(Sesamum indicum)*, soyabean *(Glycine max)*, linseed *(Linum usitatissimum)*, sunflower seed *(Helianthus annus)* etc.

6. **Fruits and nuts:** A variety of fruits and nuts are obtained from different plant species. Fruits are classified on the basis of their occurrence into tropical and temperate fruits and also on the basis of their botanical properties and contents. Major fruits of India include grapes (Vitis vinifera), banana *(Musa sapientum)*, orange *(Citrus sinensis)*, coconut *(Cocos nucifera)*, apple *(Malus pumila)*, mango *(Mangifera indica)*, pear *(Pyrus communis)*, peach *(Prunus persica)*, pineapple *(Ananas comosus)*, lemons *(Citrus* species), dates *(Phoenix dactylifera)*, etc. In addition to these there are some less important fruits in terms of their commercial importance. Important nuts include cashew-nut *(Anacardium occidentale)*, chestnuts *(Castanea* sepcies), walnut *(Juglans regia)*, almod *(Prunus dulcis)*, etc.

7. **Vegetables:** Vegetables are classified on the basis of their useful parts such as leafy vegetable, fruit vegetable, roots, and underground stems. These are the sources of different vitamins and minerals. Important vegetables are root crops such as potato *(Solanum tuberosum)*, sweet potato *(Ipomoea batatus)*, yams *(Dioscorea* spp.), colocasia *(Colocasia* spp.), onion *(Allium cepa)*, beet root *(Beta*

vulgaris), garlic *(Allium sativum),* turnip *(Brassica rapa),* carrot *(Daucus carrota)*, radish *(Raphanus sativus),* etc., leafy vegetables such as cabbage, cauliflower *(Brassica oleracea),* lettuce *(Lactuca sativa),* spinach *(Spinacia oleracea),* etc., and fruit and seed vegetables such as cucurbits (pumpkins, *Cucurbita* spp.; bottle gourd, *Lagenaria vulgaris;* watermelon, *Citrullus* spp *Cucumis* spp.; *Luffa* spp.) chillies *(Capsicum spp.),* tomato *(Lycopersicon esculentum),* brinjal *(Solanum melongena),* lady's finger *(Abelmoschus esculentus),* etc.

8. **Spices, condiments and other flavourings:** Spices are aromatic vegetable products used in powdered state. They have strong odour sweet or bitter taste. Condiments on the other hand are spices or other flavourings having a sharp taste and are usually added to food after cooking. Spices and condiments include ginger *(Zingiber officinale),* turmeric *(Curcuma longa),* cinnamon *(Cinnamomum verum),* clove *(Eugenia caryophyllus),* saffron *(Crocus sativus),* black pepper *(Piper nigrum),* cardamom (smaller) *(Elletaria cardamomum),* coriander *(Coriandrum sativum),* fennel *(Foenculum vulgare),* cumin *(Cuminum cyminum),* etc.

9. **Fumitory and masticatory materials:** These include stimulants, narcotics and other hallucinogenic materials obtained from plants. These include tobacco *(Nicotiana tabacum),* hemp *(Cannabis sativa),* etc.

10. **Beverages:** These include alcoholic and non-alcoholic beverages. Alcoholic beverages are obtained by distillation of fruits, and other plant parts containing sugars, whereas non-alcoholic beverages are tea *(Camellia sinensis)* and coffee *(Coffea arabica).* Cocoa *(Theobroma cacao)* is another non-alcoholic beverage.

11. **Wood:** Commercial wood or timber is one of the most important use of plants. The quality of wood is determined in terms of their resistance against decay or insect and fungal attacks, strength, weight, elasticity and durability. Woods are used in different ways such as in the construction of houses and buildings, as fuel, containers and in the manufacture of tool handles and other instruments. Most

important timber of India are sal (*Shorea robusta),* teak *(Tectona grandis), shisham* (Dalbergia sissoo), decodar *(Cedrus deodara),* siris *(Albizzia* spp) etc.

12. **Tannins and dyes:** Important tannin yielding plants are *Acacia mearnsii* (black wattle), red mangrove *(Rhizophora mangle),* sicilian sumac *(Rhus coriaria),* etc. Vegetable dyestuffs are obtained from annatoo *(Bixa orellana),* safflower *(Carthamus tinctorius),* indigo *(Indigofera* spp.) henna *(Lawsonia inermis),* etc.

13. **Rubber yielding plants:** Some of the plants yield latex which is processed as rubber. Rubber yielding plants include para rubber (*Hevea* species) and its substitutes such as ceara rubber *(Manihot glaziovii),* castilla rubber *(Castilla elastica),* India or Assam rubber *(Ficus elastica),* etc.

14. **Medicinal plants:** Various parts of some plants are of medicinal importance. These are used to cure a number of ailments and disease. Important medicinal plants of India are belladona *(Atropa belladona),* quinine tree *(Cinchona* spp.), aconite *(Aconitum napellus),* ephedrine *(Ephedra* spp.), opium poppy *(Papaver somniferum),* rauwolfia or sarpgandha *(Rauvolfia serpentina),*ergot *(Claviceps purpurea),*etc.

ENDANGERED FLORA OF INDIA AND ITS CONSERVATION

The increase of human population in the last few decades demanding development in various spheres has caused directly or indirectly a lot of disturbances in natural ecosystems. The growth of large urban areas, construction activities such as dams, buildings and roads, encroachment on vast areas of forest lands for extension of arable expanses and mining operations are examples of direct onslaughts on nature which has steadily depleted natural resources. Thus, there are a number of causes of threat to plant species. The following are the important causes of threat to plant species:

1 Increasing urbanisation.

2 Development activities such as Hydro-electric Projects and River Valley Projects.

3 Road construction.

4 Mining and indiscriminate explosions.
5 Extension of agricultural areas.
6 Pollution resulting from urbanisation, industrialisation.
7 Excessive use of chemical fertilizers and pesticides.

In 1968 at an international Conference of UNESCO, the problem of conservation of flora was discussed and several recommendations were made urging the International Biological Programme (IBP), the International Union for Conservation of Nature and Natural Resources (IUCN) and various national and international organisations to initiate studies into these problems including the protection and preservation of wild fauna and flora in their natural habitats/ecosystem by establishing the natural reserves.

IUCN reviewed the endangered species acts proposed by USA (1973) and UK (1975). The year 1970 was declared and observed as **European Conservation Year** by the Council of Europe urging the member states to promote and encourage conservation programmes.

India promulgated the Wild Life (protection) Act in the year 1972. But it did not include any plants in the lists of scheduled protected species. Red Data Books have been published by IUCN to list the endangered plants throughout the world. It is estimated that out of 3 lakhs species of plants in the world, over 20,000 are in the category of either endangered or vulnerable.

In India, the real threat to plant species lies especially in areas which are subjected to considerable development activities, *e.g.*, forests which lie close to villages and breadth of the Himalaya, the Western and Eastern Ghats of peninsular India, the Vindhya and Satpura Hill ranges, and densely forested hilly regions in Assam, Nagaland, Meghalaya, Manipur and Mizoram in Eastern India. These regions incidentally abound in many tourist spots and pilgrimage centres, which attract large number of people who damage to the flora. Besides the threatened species, there are some *endemic* species also, which are restricted to a particular locality or region. The endemism may also be caused by natural or biotic factors. Some of the medicinal plants have become threatened due to their over-exploitation in trade.

Endangered Plants

In India, nearly 1000 plant species have been identified as endangered, threatened or rare. A list of some most conspicuous species in different parts of the country is given below:

	Plant Species	Family
1	*Abies delavayi*	Pinaceae
2	*Acanthephippium sytheiense*	Orchidaceae
3	*Aconitum deinorrhzum*	Ranunculaceae
4	*Adinandra griffithii*	Theaceae
5	*Aglaia perviridis*	Mejiaceae
6	*Amblyanthus multiflorus*	Myrsananceae
7	*Anacolosa ilicoides*	Oleaceae
8	*Anoectolchilus sikkimensis*	Orchidaceae
9	*Angiopteris erecta*	Angiopteridaceae
10	*Aphyllorchis montana*	Orchidaceae)
11	*Arachnanthe cathcartii*	Orchidaceae
12	*A. clarkei*	Orchidaceae
13	*Artemisia amygdolina*	Asteraceae
14	*Arundina grammifolia*	Orchidaceae
15	*Astragakys strobiliferus*	Paoilionaceae
16	*Atropa acuminata*	Solanaceae
17	*Balanophora dioica*	Balanophoraceae
18	*Botrychium virginianum*	Ophioglossaceae
19	*Brainae insignis*	Blechnaceae
20	*Camellia caduca*	Theaceae
21	*Catamixis baccharoides*	Asteraceae
22	*Colchicum luteum*	Lilaceae
23	*Captis leeta*	Ranunceae
24	*Cythea gigantea*	Cyatheaceae
25	*Cymbidium macrorhizon*	Orchidaceae

26	*Cypripedium Cordigerum*	Orchidaceae
27	*Cypripedium elegans*	Orchidaceae
28	*Cypripedium himalacicum*	Orchidaceae
29	*Cypripedium macranthobn*	Orchidaceae
30	*Dendrobium densiflorum*	Orchidaceae
31	*Dianthus coschemiricus*	Caryophyllaceae
32	*Didiciea cunningnamii*	Orchidaceae
33	*Dioscorea deltoidea*	Dioscoreaceae
34	*Dipteris wallichii*	Dipteridaceae
35	*Dischudua benghalensis*	Asclepiadaceae
36	*D. raflesiana*	Aclepiadaceae
37	*Drosera indica*	Droseraceae
38	*D. burmanni*	Droseraceae
39	*Elaeocarpus prunifolius*	Elaeocarpaceae
40	*Eremostachys superba*	Lamiaceae
41	*Eria crassicaulis*	Orchidaceae
42	*Galeola lindleyana*	Orchidaceae

3

The Wild-Life in India

The term wild-life has different meanings for different people. For a common man, wildl-ife means the whole lot of undomesticated animals who live in their natural habitat such as forests, grasslands etc. However, Gee (1964) in his book entitled "Wild-Life of India" has said "the term wild-life embraces all living creatures and implies their conservation". According to the Wild-life Society, Washington, "wild-life includes all wild vertebrates and larger invertebrates important from aesthetic, sporting, utilitarian and nuisance stand point". The Indian Wild-life (Protection) Act, 1972 defines wild-life as "Wild-life includes any animal, bees, butterflies, crustecea, fish and moths, and aquatic and land vegetation which forms part of any habitat".

Wild-life of India is a great natural heritage. It is estimated that about 4-5 per cent of all known plant and animal species on the earth are found in India. This includes about 13 thousand species of flowering plants, 50 thousand species of insects, 4 thousand species of molluscs, 6,500 species of other invertebrates, 2 thousand species of fishes, 140 species of amphibians, 420 species of reptiles, 1200 species of birds and 320 species of mammals.

The main reason for this remarkable diversity of live forms in a single country is the great diversity of ecosystems, which this country has preserved and supported through the ages on account of wide geographical and climatological variations through out the length and width of the country. Almost every type of habitat is found in India ranging from Alpine Meadows and temperate forests to tropical rain forests, cold to hot deserts, moist and dry deciduous forests to marshes, wetlands, mangroves and marine ecosystems. Protection of wild-life and environment has been part of our ethos and is well reflected in our scriptures and mythology. It is the proud privilege of India to claim that the world's first recorded conservation measures specifically for wildlife were enacted in India in the third century B. C. particularly in the days of emperor Ashoka.

Despite our rich traditions, we have witnessed serious depletion of our biological heritage under the pressures exerted by the phenomenan increase in our human and live stock population. It is now widely recognized that the management of forest areas of the country with the sole objective of preservation of flora and fauna, is neither practical nor possible, at least in near future. Keeping this in view, the National Wild-life Action Plan adopted by the Indian Board for Wild Life under the Chairmanship of Late Prime Minister Smt. Indira Gandhi in 1982, emphasised the need for establishment of a network of wildlife reserves representing all the biographic zones of the country for conservation of flora and fauna.

As a follow-up action of the National Wild-life Action Plan, the Wild-life Institute of India, Dehradun, carried out a detailed survey of forest regions in the country and published a report "Planning a Wildlife Protected Area Network in India" which was released by Late Prime Minister Shri Rajiv Gandhi in the meeting of Indian Board for Wild-Life held in 1988. The report recommends that at least 5 per cent of the total geographical area of the country should be brought under national parks and sanctuaries. It has been the endeavour of the Govt. of India to persuade the State Governments to implement the recommendation of wild-life institute of India and bring viable extents of all representative bio-geographic regions under the ambit of national parks and sanctuaries. Today the country has 480 sanctuaries and 80 national parks extending over an area of over 1.48 lakh Sq. Kilometre that is about 4.27% of the total geographical area of the country.

The National Forest Policy of 1988 re-emphasised the importance of environmental and ecosystem conservation and laid stress on conserving the natural heritage by preserving the vast varieties of flora and fauna which represent the remarkable biodiversity and genetic resources of the country. In the current century our approach of wild-life conservation have been of two fold. (1) Conservation of wild-life through legislation, and (2) Through intensive management of specially identified protected areas having rich biodiversity. The Indian Board for wild-life with Prime Minister of India as Chairman is apex advisory body on all the matters concerning wild-life. It advises the Centre and State Governments on ways and means of promoting conservation and on effective control of poaching. It also advises the Governments regarding setting up of protected areas, Zoos and policy regarding trade of wildlife products and promotion of public interest in wildlife.

The current legislation history for protection of wild-life dates back to the year 1887 when "Wild Birds Protection Act" no. X of 1887 was enacted. This act enabled the British Government to frame rules prohibiting the possession or sale of any kind of specified wild birds. The Government in the year 1912 passeds the " Wild Birds and Animals Protection Act" no. VIII of 1912 as the Act of 1887 proved to be inadequate for the protection of wild birds and animals. This was followed by several other acts. However, a comprehensive Wild-life (Protection) Act was enacted in 1972, which provides the main legal framework for present day conservation and protection of wild-life in India. The two main objectives of the Act are to provide protection to the endangered species listed in the schedules of the Act and to provide legal support to the conservation areas of the country classified as national parks, sanctuaries and closed areas. Incidental to the above objectives, it also regulates trade in wild-life species. This

Act has been comprehensively amended in 1991 making punishments more stringent and has also made provisions for protection of specified plant species and ex-situ conservation of wild animals.

Forest and wild-life is placed in the concurrent list of the constitution of India, but its main executing agencies are in the States. The main responsibility of the preservation of wild-life and the control of wildlife trade in the States vests with the Chief Wild-life Warden who is supported by Forestry and wild-life personnel designated as Wild-life Wardens and Deputy Wild-life Wardens with network of staff under their control. In the centre Director of Wild-life Preservation, who coordinates the wild-life activities in the States and contributes in the decision-making at apex level, heads wild-life organisation. Local people taking interest in wild-life conservation are also declared as Honorary Wildlife Wardens to give support to State forest administration and develop linkages with the local people. Most of the important wildlife areas are provided with Radio Telephonic Communication System, arms and ammunition and support vehicles for the mobility of staff.

Central Government is also providing assistance to State Governments for Development of National Park and Sanctuaries and special schemes like "Project Tiger (1973)" and "Project Elephant (1992)" have been launched to conserve the species and its habitat in a sustainable manner. The activities like restoration of habitat, preparation of management plan for protected areas, infrastructural support for protection and restoration of corridors of long ranging animals like elephants, educational and awareness programmes etc., are supported under the schemes.

Over the years, it was felt that the provisions of the Act were inadequate to meet the challenges posed by the poachers, illegal traders and other vested interests. The unscrupulous traders were taking advantage of the rampant poverty in the rural areas and using the tribals and other poor people for removal of wild animals, timber, firewood and other forest usufructs. However, it is realised and appreciated that merely resorting to legal remedies, problems can not be resolved and have to be worked out by providing employment to the local people in a meaningful manner and by providing alternatives to forest usufructs so that their dependence on forests is reduced. Keeping this in view, schemes like "Ecodevelopment in and Around Protected Areas" and "Association of tribals in regeneration of forests" have been initiated.

Realising the importance of ex-situ conservation, the Govt. of India, by an amendment in Wildlife (Protection) Act, 1972, made a provision for the creation of a Central Zoo Authority to oversee, monitor and coordinate the management of the Zoos in the country. The Central Zoo Authority will specify the minimum standards for the Zoos, coordinate the captive breeding programme of rare and endangered species and will also provide both technical and financial assistance to the Zoos for their development and management on scientific lines.

The commercial exploitation of rare and endangered plant species has also been brought under the purview of Wildlife (Protection) Act and export of all wild animals and articles made therefrom are prohibited under the export-import policy of the country. Several endangered plant species are also prohibited for export under the policy while for other wild plants, their products and derivatives, a No-Objection Certificate has to be procurred from the concerned jurisdictional forest officer in order to ensure that wild plant species are not over-exploited.

Keeping the Convention on Biological Diversity in view which was signed at Rio in 1992, the Ministry of Environmental and Forests has taken an initiative for drafting appropriate legislation and export control orders so as to regulate the transfer of indigenous genetic material from the country and its sustainable utilisation. This will safe guard the long term interest of the country and ensure appropriate returns from the possible use of our Biomaterial in future. The Ministry of Environment and Forests, Govt. of India has also undertaken an exercise to prepare National

Action Plan for Biodiversity Conservation, which would be finalised after extensive consultations with other Ministries, State Govt., Scientific Institutions and relevent Non-Governmental Organisation.

The role of Research on various biological and management problems relating to conservation of wild-life and imparting training to wild-life managers in the modern techniques of management cannot be over-emphasised. The Wildlife Institute of India is doing a commendable job in achieving this twin objective of training and research. The Govt. of India also encourages and partonizes wild-life research and studies from non-government organisations, universities and dedicated individuals.

Wild-life conservation has very large ambit with unbounded potentials for the well being of human kind. However, this can be achieved only when every individual understands its significance and contributes his bit. It should be the endeavour all those concerned to develop it into a mass movement where by the people themselves will develop the strategies for conservation of this great natural heritage.

REASONS FOR WILDLIFE DEPLETION

Success in evolution is measured in terms of survival, failure by extinction. Most recent extinction, however, can be imputed either directly or indirectly to man, more specifically to man's demographic and technological expansion. The majority of recent extinctions, both in plant and animals are however, attributable to environmental changes arising from alteration, degradation or destruction of natural habitats, deforestation, agriculture expansion, unrestricted grazing and spreading urbanisation. A basic consideration is the balance between mortality and reproduction. Having a naturaly low reproductive rate handicaps some of the endangered species. Under optimum condition this may be no grate disadvantage, but it can have serious repercussions if normal reproduction is thwarted by undue disturbance or by such factors as weakening of species vitality through fragmentation of the population. The depletion of wild-life is however, mainly attributable to the following factors:

1. **Habitat destruction**: With the ever increasing pressure of human population together with their domestic animals, associated with other developmental activities for the better living of mankind, the natural habitat are being destroyed. According to an estimate one hundred—thousand hectare of forest are being destroyed every year. Similarly the multipurpose project like big dams are bound to deplete a large habitable area, a large part of the land gets submerged and due to this the various plant and animal species of that area are forced to be removed or destroyed. Habitat destruction is considered as the primary reason for the extinction of most of the species.

2. **Trade in Wildlife**: The exploitation of the wild-life for the commercial purposes is only second reason for their depletion. The illegal killing and smuggling of wildlife is rampant in all most all parts of the world. It is estimated that between 1850 and 1890 approximately 47 thousands Elephant were killed annualy in Africa to supply the Ivory market of London. The cost of the tusk is about several lakhs. In India too, a wanton killing of Elephants to obtain their tusk had taken place. Poaching of male elephants for tusk leads to a disbalance in the sex ratio of their population.

The one horned Rhino is poached for its horn, which is supposed to have some aphrodisiac property. Earlier this animal was found in the tarai lands of U.P. Assam and Bengal but now confined in only one or two pockets of the country and their numbers has also decreased to two hundred to four hundred. Similarly the musk deer formerly wide spread throught the Himalayas within mountain and subalpine forest and alpine scrub, is now confined within a quarter of its former range in India. This beautiful animal is killed for a special gland or musk sac, which is found in the abdominal region of the male. Today the musk fetches arround fourty thousand to sixty thousand U.S. in the international market and about two hundred male musk deer are to be killed to obtain one kilogram of musk.

The other wild animals, which are frequently killed for their commercial value, include Tigers, Snakes, fur bearing animals etc.

3. Introduction of exotic species: Introduction of exotic species also leads to the depletion in the population of the species because the introduced species find difficult to adjust in the totally new habitat due to various climatic as well as biological factors.

4. Over grazing: Over grazing by cattle is one of the greatest factor in the degradation of the natural habitat of the wild-life. The problem of over grazing is much more in the Himalayan regions. Some times the population of cattles in an area becomes more than the population of human beings. The cattle not only compet with the wild animals for their food but also destroy many plant species at the ground level.

5. Natural Calamities: Natural Calamities are also responsible for the depletion of the wild-life. During the mansoon season in 1998 the entire Kaziranga national park in Assam was heavily flooded which led to the death of 28 Rhinos, 70-85 Deers, 8 Beers and and 3 Elephant and many plant species were also lost. Similarly the forest fires, Earthquake and landslides are other natural factors, which destroy the wild-life.

4

Status of Biodiversity in India

The Indian land mass, extending over a total area of 329 million hectare, is located between 6 ° and 38° N latitude and 69° and 97° E longitudes. Its rich biological resources are a result of India's diverse physical features and climate, and natural evolution of a variety of phytogeographic conditions. The Indian landmass, bounded by the Himalayas in the north, the Bay of Bengal in the east and the Arabian Sea in the west, consists of three well-defined regions:

(i) The Trans Himalayan mountain zones including the north-eastern hill ranges.

(ii) The Indo-Gangetic plains.

(iii) The Peninsula including the eastern and western Ghats and the Vindya-Satpura ranges.

According to world biogeographical classification, India represents two of the major realms, the palaearctic and Indo-Malayan and three biomes, tropical humid forests, tropical dry/deciduous forests and warm deserts/semi deserts. Nature has bestowed India with rich forests and wild life resources.

The Himalaya, with a total area of nearly 100 m ha, dominates the floristic estate of the entire Indian subcontinent. Flowering plants had evolved and diversified in the Late Cretaceous, and had vigorous mechanisms of dispersal compared to the plant groups that had evolved earlier. The relatively young Himalayas opened new southward routes of migration and colonization into what had hitherto been an island. At the eastern end, through the Assam gate, came the Chinese and Malayan elements. From the west came some Palaearctic and Ethiopian elements. The Himalaya acted as a two-way highway linking West Africa to South-east Asia. In the Peninsula, there may have also been a crossover point between the Southern Western Ghats and Eastern Hills. Besides being a highway for living species, the Himalaya also deflect the rain bearing clouds into the region, controlling the rainfall regime, and thence the environmental conditions and life in the subcontinent. In the Peninsula, the rainfall pattern is also governed by the Western Ghats.

Although most of the country is situated north of the tropic of cancer, India has a tropical monsoonal climate. It depends for rains on monsoon, which originates south of the Equator and on winter rain caused by western disturbances originating in the Mediterranean. India's immense biological diversity encompasses ecosystems, populations, species and their genetic make up. This diversity can be attributed to the vast varity in physiography and climatic situations resulting in a diversity of ecological habitats ranging from tropical, subtropical, temperate, alpine to desert. The Wildlife Institute of India (WII) has proposed a classification which divides the country into 10 bio geographic regions: Trans Himalayan, Himalayan, Indian Desert, Semi Arid, Western Ghats, Deccan Peninsula, Gangetic Plains, North East India, Islands and Coasts. India is one of the 12 identified mega biodiversity centers. It also has two of the 18 identified hot spots-the Eastern Himalayas and the Western Ghats.

The number of plant species is estimated to be over 45,000, representing about 7 per cent of the world's flora. These are categorised in different taxonomic divisions including over 15,00 flowering plants. Estimates for the lower plants are: 64 gymnosperms, 2843 bryophytes, 1012 pteridophytes, 1940 lichens, 12,480 algae and 23,000 fungi.

Some 4,900 species of flowering plants are endemic to the country. Among the endemic species, 2,532 species are found in the Himalaya and adjoining areas, followed by 1,782 species in Peninsular India. About 1500 endemic species are facing varying degree of threats.

The faunal wealth is equally diverse. The total number of animal species is estimated at 81,000, representing about 6.4 per cent of world's fauna. India's animal diversity includes over 5,000 molluscs and about 57,0000 insects, besides other invertebrates. There are 2,546 fish, 204 amphibians, 428 reptiles, 1228 birds and 372 mammals. The extent of endemism is very high, about 62 per cent.

Very little is known about the extent of the diversity of micro-organisms, particularly the bacteria and viruses. Consolidated data on bacteria and viruses are to be compiled. Detailed survey has to be made about the aquatic biota related to the 14 major, 44 medium and 55 minor river systems.

India is also considered one of the world's 12 centers of origin of cultivated plants. India's rich germ plasm resources includes 51 species of cereals and millets, 104 species of fruits, 27 species of spices and condiments, 55 species of vegetables and pulses, 24 species of fibre crops, 12 species of oil seeds, and various wild strains of tea, coffee, tobacco and sugarcane. There are several hundred species of wild crop relatives distributed all over the country especially in the Western and Eastern Himalayas, in the West Peninsula and the Malabar Coast, in North Eastern India, the Gangetic Plains and the Indus Plains. The ancient practice of domesticating animals has resulted in India's diverse livestock, poultry and other animal breeds. This is a significant percentage of world diversity. India's 8 breeds of buffalo represent the entire range of genetic diversity of buffalos in the world. Besides, there are 26 breeds of cattle, 40 of sheeps, 20 of goats, 8 of camels, 6 of horses, 2 of donkeys and 18 types of poultry.

THE BIOLOGICAL DIVERSITY ACT, 2002 OF INDIA

The conservation and protection of our rich biological diversity has attracted attention at all the levels in the country. India is a party to the United Nations Convention on Biological Diversity and has signed the Convention during the Earth Summit at Rio-de-Janerio on 5th of June 1992 and this convention came into force on 29th December, 1993. Accordingly for the conservation of biological diversity, sustainable use of its components and fair and equal sharing of the benefits coming out of the use of biological resources, knowledge and for all other connected purposes, The Biological Diversity Act, 2002 was passed by the Indian Parliament and has received the ascent of the President on 5th February, 2003 (No. 18 of 2003).

MAJOR RELEVANT PROVISIONS OF CENTRAL ACTS RELATING TO BIODIVERSITY

1 **Agricultural and Processed Food Products Export Development Authority Act 1985/86:**
   - Promotion and regulation of export of agricultural products specified in the Schedules-includes medicinal plants.

2 **Agricultural Produce (Grading and Marking) Act, 1937:**
   - Fixing grade designations to indicate quality of any specified agricultural produce.
   - Prohibition or restriction on trade in wrongly marked/graded produce.
   - Extension of such provisions to any other article (including non-agricultural articles).

3 **Cardamom Act, 1965:**
   - Provisions as in Rubber Act: included seeds. Provisions for prohibiting/restricting export-import of cardamom. Applicable to *Elettaria cardaromum maton,* but extandable to any other plant notified by cardamom Board.

4 **Coconut Development Board Act, 1979:**
   - As in rubber Act, Tea Act, Cardamom Act etc.

5 **Customs Act, 1962:**
   - Regulation or prohibition of import and export of specified articles.
   - Regulation of import-export specifically for:

(a) the protection of human, animal or plant life or health.
(b) the conservation of exhaustible natural resources.
(c) regulation of transportation and storage of notified items.

6 **Destructive Insects and Pests Act, 1914:**
- Prohibition or regulation of import of any articles which may cause infection to any plant.
- Prohibition or regulation of movement, between States within India, of articles likely to cause infection to any plant.

7 **Environment Protection Act, 1986:**
- General measures to protect environment.
- Restriction of industrial and other processes/ activities in specified areas.
- Prevention and control of hazardous substances, including their manufacture, use, release and movement.

8 **Fisheries Act, 1897:**
- Prohibition on use of explosive for fishing.
- Prohibition on use of poisions for fishing.
- Regulation on fishing in private waters, with consent of owners/ right holders.

9 **Forest Act, 1927:**
- Setting up of managing reserved forests.
- Setting up and managing village forests.
- Setting up and managing protected forests.
- Protection of non government forests and lands.
- Control of movement of forest produce.
- Control of grazing and trespass by cattle in forest land.

10 **Forest (conservation) Act, 1947:**
- Prohibition or regulation of no-forest use of forest land.

11 **Import and Export (Control) Act, 1947:**
- Prohibition or restriction on imports and exports of specified items.
- Regulation of transportation of specified items.

12 **Wildlife (Protection) Act, 1972:**
- Restriction or prohibition on hunting of animals.
- Protection of specified plants.
- Setting up and managing sanctuaries and national parks.
- Setting up of zoo authority, control of zoos and captive breeding.
- Control of trade and commerce in wild animals, animal articles and trophies.

FOLLOW UP ACTION IN INDIA AFTER EARTH SUMMIT

The Convention on Biological Diversity is a revolutionary document of far reaching significance that envisages a reciprocity of arrangements between developed and developing countries to ensure a more harmonious, secure and sustainable future through conserving and sustainable utilisation of the biological wealth of our planet. However, the ultimate result of this Convention would depend upon the follow up and implementations. The Ministry of Environment and Forests, which is the nodal unit in the Central Government for issues related to the Convention has set into motion several follow up actions.

Subsequent to the signing of the Convention by India, extensive consultations were organised at the national and state levels to analyse the implications of the provisions of the convention. As a result, 50 action points were identified for implementation at national, state and local levels. Of these, 26 action points require the active participation of NGOs for their implementation.

The Ministry of Environment and Forests had constituted nine expert groups for preparing reports in order to accelerate the process of conservation and sustainable use of natural resources through programmes on scientific lines. These groups cover the following specific areas:

- Survey, identification and monitoring
- In situ conservation
- Ex situ conservation

- Sustainable use
- Access to and transfer of technology
- Research, training and cooperation
- Legal measures
- Strengthening impact assessment measures.

In addition a comprehensive status report on biological diversity in India is under preparation, since as of now no such report is available for the country. The Indian Institute of Public Administration is compiling the status report, which would cover the various facetes of biodiversity conservation, for the Ministry. The report is in two volumes, volume 1 contains an overview of the staus of biological diversity in India, as also the broad strategy for its conservation. The second volume, which is in three parts, contains texts of the papers contributed by various agencies and experts.

An analysis of 24 existing central laws relevent to biological diversity has revealed that there are significant gaps to the existing legal and regulatory measures. Keeping in view the provisions of the Convention, the main elements for inclusion in a comprehensive act on biodiversity are being identified following deliberations with the concerned Ministries, Departments and Government and Non-Government agencies. In the light of the provisions of the Convention, deep concern has been expressed over the free movement of genetic material from our country, which continues unhindered in the absence of a comprehensive legal framework to regulate it. Since the regular enactment on biodiversity would take some time, it was considered appropriate to undertake immediate steps to regulate the transfer of genetic material. The Ministry has initiated an exercise for formulation of National Action Plan on Biodiversity, for which a core group of experts has been constituted. A detailed frame work of Action Plan has been prepared and the various action points have been categorised into the following five major groups for which identified experts are preparing the Action Plan:

- Documentation, conservation, research and monitoring.
- Sustainable utilisation, public participation and benefit sharing.
- Formulation of policy and planning generating finances.
- Instituting building activities, technology development programme and human resource development.
- Legal measures and biosaftey.

Keeping in view the fact that many components of biological diversity are common among neighbouring countries as natural ecosystems are spread over political boundries, and that several of the floral and faunal species are endemic to this region, the Ministry of Environment and Forests with support from UNEP had organised an official level meeting among SAARC, ASEAN and other countries of the region.

India had earlier contributed significantly in the seven intergovernmental sessions for negotiating the Convention on Biological Diversity prior to the Rio conference. Subsequently, Indian delegations have participated actively in the two sessions of the Intergovernmental Committee on the Biological Diversity (ICCBD), held in Geneva in October 1993 and in Nairobi in June 1994, for preparing the first meeting of Conference of Parties (COP) held in Nassau, the Bahamas from 28 November to 9 December 1994. Since then many more meetings have held and the latest was in New Delhi in 2002.

PEOPLE'S PARTICIPATION IN BIOLOGICAL DIVERSITY CONSERVATION

India has a rich tradition of people's participation and folk practices for the conservation of biodiversity. The symbiotic relationship between folk traditions and modern scientific institutes needs to be enhanced to enrich both. It is recognised that effective conservation can take place only if there are effective and equitable ways of using the components of biodiversity in a sustainable manner, and ways of sharing the benefits accruing from conservation of biodiversity with local communities. There is increasing consciousness of the fact that such conservation with sustainable use is possible only with the involvement and co-operation of local communities in the effort, and for this the development of institutional structures at local and other levels is necessary. Some of these are as under:

- **Towards the utilisation of components of biodiversity**

The sustainable use of components of biodiversity in all sectors, including agriculture, animal husbandry, fisheries, forestry, industry and other economic activities needs to be promoted.

Traditional and other folk uses of biodiversity components, which are ecologically sustainable, need to be revived and encouraged.

Technological and other means to achieve efficient and sustainable use of biodiversity components, including access to appropriate technologies from outside the country, must be promoted and developed. Measures to minimise and eliminate unsustainable utilisation of biodiversity components need to be initiated.

- **Towards sharing of benefits**

Equitable access to biodiversity, keeping in mind the interest of national sovereignty and the rights of local communities, needs to be ensured. The equitable distribution of benefits arising from the use of biodiversity components, in particular guaranteeing fair returns to traditional communities, and continuing contribution to the conservation, development, and maintenance of biodiversity must also be ensured. Means of ensuring that a share of the benefits from the commercial utilisation of biodiversity components is guaranteed as return to local communities, for their continuing conservation, development and maintenance of biodiversity must be found.

Measures must be taken to gain access to the

biodiversity held in the national and international ex-situ collections, especially in the case of germ plasm taken from India and stored outside, and to a share of the benefits being generated from the international use of this germ plasm. Measures at bilateral, regional and international levels, to ensure that benefits generated by the transfer of genetic material are equitably distributed, and the countries of origin are adequately rewarded also need to be taken.

- **Towards strengthening institutional structures**

Appropriate institutional structures at local, state and national levels, for the purpose of carrying out the necessary actions need to be created, encouraged or revived.

The net work of research and monitoring agencies and individuals, both governmental and non-governmental, and involving both formal and folk knowledge systems, to ensure the implementation of the actions suggested, specially under documentation, research and monitoring, needs to be created. A decentralized cadre of formal and folk taxonomists and ecologists needs to be developed and encouraged to carry out exercise of mapping, inventorying, and monitoring of biodiversity, especially by promoting a symbiotic relationship between formal and folk systems. Structures for participatory management of protected areas and other conservation areas, involving as equal partners, government agencies and local communities, and as supportive partners non-governmental organisations and independent scientific and cultural institutions, must also be created.

Coordinating mechanisms for institutional structures at local, state and national levels, with the aim of promoting conservation and sustainable use of biodiversity, need to be initiated and encouraged. It is also very important to consolidate the national, state and local level database. These would be used both for information storage, as also to act as nodal bio resource centres for information dissemination and other relevant activities. Their creation and management should ensure co-ordination and complementariness between the repositories, full public participation, and respect for the informal knowledge system. A network of biodiversity conservation and sustainable use extension workers, for the purpose of carrying out the actions needs to be created.

MONITORING OF NATURAL RESOURCES

The occurrence and abundance of any organism in a given environment depends on a number of conditions. In nature, the distribution of animals and plants is controlled by the quantity and variability of materials necessary for the organism, and the physical factors and the limit of tolerance of the organisms to these components of the environment. The various factors of environment do not exert equal influence on an organism in a particular situation. An environmental factor, which is critical or limiting to one organism, may leave another in the same environment unaffected. Monitoring is very essential and in the present times it has also become fashionable to monitor each and every activity especially in the business. Monitoring is always purpose oriented and tells us how something is changing, it is repeated at regular intervals and it often provides the baseline for recording possible change in the future. It is a dynamic in philosophy; purpose oriented and needs to be critically examined prior to implementation. By definitation a monitoring programme must have clear objectives. Most of them fall in the following groups:

- To record long term environmental changes and its ecological effects.
- To record response to a change management factor such as drainage, grazing, use of herbicides or agricultural intensification.
- To record rate of change such as decline of a rare species or habitat.
- To determine the effect of a form of management or to determine and reduce costs.

While selecting a monitoring programme there are a variety of constraints that have to be taken into consideration, such as:

- Long-term directional changes being complicated by normal seasonal and annual cycles.
- Irregular and natural fluctuations, which may mask the features of interest.
- Ecosystems and species adjusting to current and recent management specially when discontinued or changed.
- Adjustment or relaxation to historical changes such as drainage, fire and clear cutting of forests.
- Successional changes which can be either directional or cyclical.

Monitoring is still often used in a very broad sense; however, the design of a monitoring strategy is generally assisted by the adoption of clearer definitions, which are as follows:

(a) **Survey:** It is an exercise in which a set of qualitative or quantitative observations are made, usually by means of a standard procedure and within a restricted period of time, but without any preconce-ption of what findings ought to be.

(b) **Surveillance:** An extended programme of survey, undertaken in order to provide a time series, to ascertain the variability and range of states or values, which might be encountered over time.

(c) **Monitoring:** Intermittent regular or irregular surveillance carried out in order to ascertain the extent of compliance with a predetermined standard or the degree of deviation from an expected norm.

5

Case Study Insect Diversity in a High Altitude Forest

To maintain the rich biological diversity of the Indian Himalayan Region, a protected area of networks has been established and the biodiversity rich areas have been conserved as wildlife sanctuaries, national parks and biosphere reserves. The Biosphere Reserves form an important part of our strategy to conserve the total biodiversity existing in an area, and is an important tool, which can contribute meaningfuly by involving local communities. The Nanda Devi Biosphere Reserve represents the highland zones of Himalaya comprising of several peaks like Nanda Devi, Trishul, Changbang, Dunagiri etc. Till 1939, the Nanda Devi basin was open to mountaineering and treaking, which resulted in the disturbances in the prestine ecosystem of the area rich in unique flora and fauna. In 1939 the Government of India decleared the Nanda Devi Basin as Nanda Devi Sanctuary. And its status was further elevated as Nanda Devi National Park in 1982. In 1988 the Government of India decleared the Nanda Devi Natioinal Park and its buffer areas as Nanda Devi Biosphere Reserve under the Man And Biosphere Programe of UNESCO.

Nanda Devi biosphere reserve is one of the least disturbed reserves, as no human habitation exists in the core zone of the reserve. People of two ethenic groups, Indo-

Mongoloid and Indo-Aryan origin mostly inhabit the villages, which are 47 in number and distributed in three districts. Mounteneering and trekking activities in the area were restricted from 1981 till 2003. Since 1935 when Tilman and Shipton (1936) who were the first two pioneers and tracked a way upto the Rishi Ganga gorge to the foot of the Nanda devi mountain, several naturalists and scientists have visited the area for studying the various aspects of the reserve. The present case study was carried out in the Chamoli district of Nanda Devi Biosphere Reserve during 1998-2000. The objectives of the study were:

1. Study of the abiotic factors of selected study sites which included.
   (a) Atmospheric temperature.
   (b) Humidity.
2. Physico-chemical parameters of Soil including:
   (a) Soil temperature.
   (b) Soil humidity.
   (c) Soil pH.
   (d) Soil water holding capacity
   (e) Estimation of soil organic matter.
3. Study of floristic composition of selected study sites.
4. Collection of the entomofauna and determination of their systematics.
5. Determination of trophic structure of aboveground insects collected from the study sites.
6. Construction of energy budget of the dominant grasshopper species from the study site.

MATERIAL AND METHODS STUDY AREA

Nanda Devi Biosphere Reserve is spread in three districts of newly created Uttaranchal State. The three districts include Pithoragarh and Bageshwar in Kumaun region and Chamoli in Garhwal region. It covers an area of 2,236.74 Km^2 with a core zone and a buffer zone of 624.62 and 1612.1 Km2, respectively. The buffer zone encircles the core zone and, is open for multiple uses. The people living in peripheral areas of buffer zone are allowed to use the resources to meet their daily needs. The inhabitants mostly belonging to Indo-Mongoloid and Indo-Aryan groups also practice the traditional altitudinal migration. The Biosphere has large altitudinal range varying between 1900 to 7, 817m. Most of the area of the reserve is too high to support permanent plant growth. Forest forms very little of the flora of NDBR and is restricted to Rishi gorge and along the Dhauli Ganga and Pinder valley. The area under forest is only 8% of the total geographical area of the reserve, of which only 2.9% of the area falls under dense forest having > 40% cover, according to a report of Forest Survey of India(1987-90) 92 % of the reserve is non forest including water bodies.

Selection of Study Sites in Nanda Devi Biosphere Reserve (NDBR)

Four study sites were selected in the buffer zone (Special use area) of Nanda Devi Biosphere Reserve (30° 17'-30° 40'N lattitudes and 79° 40'- 80° 05' E longitudes). The study sites were selected in a manner that they represent different kinds of vegetation and level of disturbances within the Biosphere Reserve gives location of different study sites within NDBR. The different sites selected for the collection and study purposes are as under:

Site-1. Raini: This study site is approximately 3.5 km away from the main highway, with close vicinity to the Rishi Ganga river and at an altitude of 2100 meters. Rishi Ganga makes the North-West Himalayan boundary of the Nanda Devi Biosphere Reserve. It has great mountainous slopes with sub-alpine vegetation. This part of buffer area is almost free from anthropogenic disturbances and vegetation is mainly dominated by the Surai (*Cupressus torolosa*) and a variety of herbs, shrubs, ferns and entire area was covered by thick layer of mosses.

Site-2. Tolma: A piece of three hectare forest was selected at Tolma area of NDBR, which lies in the North-west part of the Nanda Devi biosphere reserve at an altitude of 2700 m. The study area is located at a distance of 4.5 Km from the Suarithota-Joshimath Neetipass highway. This study area is highly disturbed due to the traditional altitudinal migration of Indo-Mongoloid Bhotia tribes. During their summer settlements inside the buffer zone of the biosphere reserve, the area is being used for grazing sheep, cattle and collecting fodder, fuel and medicinal plants, which are being used traditionally since centuries. This study area has a sparse plant cover.

Site-3. Dunagiri: This study site is an undisturbed area, adjacent to the core zone of the biosphere reserve and at an altitude of 3800 meter. This study area represents to a moist alpine shrub forest. The dominant species of the vegetation is Birch (*Betula utilis*) trees. This part of the biosphere reserve receives snow starting from November and snow can be seen there till the end of March. This site is located approximately 10 km. away from the Niti pass highway, main motarable approach road to the area. All the study sites are located within a distance of 26 km. in the buffer zone of Nanda Devi Biosphere Reserve.

Photo plates 35-38 show views of different study sites selected for this case study

STUDY OF ABIOTIC PARAMETERS

The temperature and humidity of the area were recorded on each sampling date with the help of thermo-hygrometer and soil thermometer. The pH. Organic matter and water holding capacity of the soil were determined on monthly basis and for this purpose soil samples from selected study sites were collected and brought to the laboratory and each parameter mentioned above was determined as per the prescribed standard method given in Michael (1984).

Biotic Factors

(A) **Analysis of Vegetation** : A detailed survey of each of the study site was carried out in order to find out the composition of the vegetation and the herbarium of the plants, which could not be identified in the field, were prepared and got identified with the help of Botanical Survey of India, Dehradun, Department of Botany, Govt. P.G. College, Rishikesh and Scientists from G.B. Pant Institute of Himalayan Environment and Development, Kosi, Almora.

(B) Collection of insects: The insects were collected by "Sweep sampling method". Net sweeps were carried out to collect the insects. The nets used in systematic sweeping were made of thick cotton clothes with a diameter of 30 cm. at the mouth and a bag length of 60 cm. Sweep sampling was done as per Gadagkar *et.al.*, 1990. For carrying out net sweeps, each study site was divided into 100 quadrates measuring 10 x 10 meter each. Ten such quadrate were chosen at random and the entire area was covered during the sweeping. Sampling was done at an interval of 30 days between 8.00 to 13.00 hours. The collected insects were transferred into bottles containing Ethly Acetate soaked cotton. These bottles were brought to the laboratory and the insects were separated according to there systematic position, stretched, pinned and oven dried at 60°C for 72 hour in order to preserve them. The species, which could not be identified in the laboratory, were sent to Zoological Survey of India, Entomological Section of FRI, Dehra dun and Indian Agricultural Research Institute, Pusa, New Delhi for their identification.

(C) Determination of Trophic Structure : Trophic structure of insects collected was determined on the basis of their feeding habits. Insects, once identified were placed in three different trophic levels *viz.*, herbivores, predators and saprophagous.

(D) Construction of Energy budget : The energy budget of *Xenocatantops karnyi* K. (a dominant grasshopper species of the study area) was studied in the laboratory. 3rd instar nymphs were collected from the study site and fed with grasses to determine the food consumption, assimilation and tissue growth rates. The insects were brought to the laboratory in

Hardwar, they were maintained in 0.1 m3 cages at a temperature of 32 ± 2°C and at an ambient relative humidity of 72%. *Cynodon dectylon* (L) Pers. was collected from the forest close to University campus on a regular basis and used as food for the grasshoppers. The grass was kept fresh by placing them in plastic tubes, which were closed to prevent insect faeces from falling into them. Energy parameters of 1st and 2nd instars were not studied because of the difficulties of handling these small nymphs and accurately measuring their food consumption. The grasshoppers were restricted from food and water for 30 minutes before the start of experiment to allow the passage of residual faeces from the gut.

Before the start of experiment, each grasshopper was weighed and individually kept in a 500 ml glass jar. At each development stage, ten grasshoppers of each sex were allowed to feed on portion of pre-weighed grass for 24 hours. After this period, the remaining grass and faeces were collected and oven dried to a constant weight at 80°C. A wet/dry mass ratio was determined for the grass and the amount ingested by each grasshopper was estimated. Dry weight equivalents of grasshoppers were also calculated by using oven drying 50 grasshoppers. Food consumption was calculated as the difference between the initial weight of the grass and weight of the grass left at the end of experiment after 24 hours. Net assimilation was calculated by subtracting the dry weight of the faecal matter from the consumed grass, while the increase in body weight was taken as a measure of tissue growth. Ecological efficiencies were calculated using Waldbauer's (1968) expression:

$$\text{Apparent Digestibility} = \frac{\text{Assimilation}}{\text{Consumption}} \times 100$$

$$\text{Efficiency of Conversion of Digested Food} = \frac{\text{Tissue Growth}}{\text{Assimilation}} \times 100$$

Results

Results on the different abiotic and biotic parameters of the present case study have been given as under:

Abiotic Factors

(A) Atmospheric Temperature and Humidity: Climatically, the study area (Nanda Devi Biosphere Reserve) is dry with low annual precipitation. The core zone of the reserve remains snow covered almost for six months of the year, except May to October. However, the buffer area, particularly the study sites receive snow only during winter. The whole year is divided into three distinct seasons, winter season (November to February), summer season (March to June) and rainy seasons (July to October).

During the first year of study (1998-1999) temperature varied from 8°C (13.02.99) to 24°C (14.06.99) in site no. 1. In site no. 2 minimum temperature recorded was 6°C on 16.12.98 and maximum temperature recorded was 26°C on 15.06.99. In site no. 3 the minimum temperature was 5°C recorded on 15.02.99 while the maximum 23°C recorded on 16.06.99. In site no. 4 the minimum and maximum temperature recorded were 4°C (16.02.99) and 22°C (18.06.99) respectively.

During second year of study (1999-2000) temperature varied from 3.5°C (13.02.2000) to 25°C (16.06.2000), 3°C (14.02.2000) to 24.5° C (17.06.2000), 2°C (15.02.2000) to 23°C (18.06.2000), 1.5°C (16.02.2000) to 22°C (19.06.2000) in site no. 1, 2, 3 and 4, respectively.

During third year of study (2000-2001) temperature varied from 4°C (15.02.2001) to 22°C (18.04.2001), 4°C (16.02.2001) to 17°C (19.04.2001), 3°C (17.02.2001) to 16°C (21.04.0001) and 2.5°C (18.02.2001) to 10°C (22.04.2001) in site no. 1, 2, 3 and 4, respectively.

Humidity ranged between 20% (15.04.99) to 88% (13.07.99) in site no. 1, from 18% (14.02.99) to 66% (19.07.99) in site no. 2, from 23% (16.11.98) to 57% (16.08.99) iy site no. 3 and from 22% (18.06.99) to 63% (17.08.99) in site no. 4 during 1998-1999. During 1999-2000 humidity varied from 21% (15.03.2000) to 82% (15.08.2000), 30% (14.11.99) to 70 (14.02.2000), 26% (15.11.99) to 67% (15.02.2000), 35% (16.10.2000) to 75% (16.02.2000) in site no. 1, 2 p3,and 4, respectively.

During 2000-2001, humidity varied from 22% (16.03.2001) to 48% (15.02.2001), 32% (14.11.200) to 48% (19.04.2001), 30% (15.11.2000) to 46% (17.02.2001) and 30% (21.03.2001) to 42% (18.02.2001) in site no. 1, 2, 3 and 4, respectively.

Temperature is the most important abiotic factors, which acts on insects directly in a variety of ways. The movement of body, respiration circulation, digestion, development of their eggs, larvae etc., depend upon the external temperature. With that of temperature, humidity and rainfall also affect the insect life. The water content of body and the moisture content of the atmosphere are among the fundamental necessities of the life. Rainfall is closely bound up with atmospheric humidity. It is not only the abundance of rainfall, but the distribution of rain in the year which is a deciding factor on the distribution and abundance of insects. According to Mani (1968), "the effect of rainfall on insects is extremely varied, some insects are unable to lay eggs until after the rains, while in some other insects emergence is possible only after the rains. A favourable effect of rainfall was noted by Reddy and Alfred (1977), who reported a highly positive correlation between the total monthly rainfall and the abundance of different groups of chewing and mining insects in Asian forest ecosystem.

(B) Physico Chemical Parameters of soil: The values of soil parameter *viz.*, soil temperature, soil moisture, water holding capacity, pH and organic matter were recorded on each month for all the four sites in the study areas during the study period.

During 1998-1999, soil temperature ranged between 4°C (Feb.) to 19°C (June), 3.8°C (Feb.) to 17.4°C (June), 3.0°C (Feb) to 16.2°C (May) and 2.1°C (Feb.) to 15°C (June) in site no. 1, 2, 3 and 4, respectively, while during 1999-2001 it varied from 1.8°C (Feb.) to 18.5°C (June), 1.4°C (Feb.) to 15.6°C (June), 0°C (Feb.) to 15°C (June) and 0°C (Feb.) to 14.4°C (June) in site no. 1,2, 3 and 4, respectively.

Soil moisture varied from 8.15% (June) to 16.3% (July), 6.3% (April) to 14.2% (July), 13.01% (Dec.) to 20.24% (July) and 10.2% (April) to 19.20% (Aug.) during 1998-1999 in site no. 1, 2, 3 and 4 respectively. Whereas it varied from 8.14% (June) to 14.6% (July), 7.89% (April) to 13.81% (July), 8.20% (April) to 19.45% (Feb.) and 10.09% (June) to 21.36% (Mar.) in site no. 1, 2, 3 and 4, respectively during 1999-2001.

During 1998-1999, water holding capacity varied from 42% (Dec.) to 52.1% (May), 41% (Dec.) to 50.3% (April), 43.8% (Nov.) to 58% (June) and 38.7% (Oct) to 44% (Dec.) in site no. 1, 2, 3 and 4, respectively, while it varied from 43.5% (Mar.) to 48% (Aug.), 40.6% (Mar.) to 47% (Oct.), 44.4% (Dec.) to 56% (May) and 40% (Aug.) to 49.8% (June) in site 1, 2, 3 and 4 respectively during 1999-2001.

The soil pH varied from 5.9 to 6.4 in site no. 1, 6.1 to 6.6 in site no. 2, 6.1 to 6.6 in site no. 3 and 6.3 to 6.7 in site no. 4 during 1998-1999, while it ranged between 6.3 to 6.6 in site no. 1, 6.4 to 6.7 in site no. 2, 6.4 to 6.7 in site no. 3 and 6.4 to 6.8 in site no. 4 during 1999-2001.

During 1998-1999, organic matter of soil varied from 4.04% (Aug.) to 6.28% (Oct.), 1.03% (July) to 1.41% (Oct.), 6.73% (Aug.) to 7.97% (Dec.) and 0.84% (July) to 1.10% (Oct.) in site no. 1, 2, 3 and 4, respectively during 1998-1999, whereas during 1999-2000, it varied from 5.14 (July) to 6.71% (Nov.), 0.96% (Sep.) to 1.16% (Oct.), 6.09% (July) to 7.55% (Nov.) and 0.93% (July) to 1.12% (Dec.) in site no. 1, 2, 3 and 4 respectively.

Biotic Factors

Vegetational Composition: The Western Himalayas is one of the well-defined and better-known Phytogeographical regions of the Indian subcontinent. Floristic composition is the major anatomical characters of the plant community. Thus a detailed survey of the vegetation was made in each study site during the study period (1998-2001).

Site-1 (Raini): In this site a total of 37 species of plants were recorded during the study period, which included 10 species of trees, 13 species of shrub and 14 species of herbs. *Cupressus Torolosa* D. Doon followed by *Poplus ciliata* Wall ex mainly dominated this part of Biosphere Reserve. Royle, *Lyonia ovalifolia* (Wall), *Plectoranthus coesta, Rumex hastatus* D. Don, *Hippophae salicifolia* D. Don and *Dexmodium elegans* D. C. The ground vegetation of this site was dominated by *Apluda mutica* L., *Cynodon dectylon* (L.) Pers, *Origanum vulgare* L., *Sporoplus* sp. and *Canabis sativa* L.

Site-2 (Lata): A total of 47 species of plants were reported from this study site, which included 8 species of trees, 14 species of shrubs and 25 species of herbs during 1998-2001. This part of study area is mainly dominated by evergreen *Cedrus deodara* (Roxb) Loud., followed by *Alnus nepalensis* Don, *Aesculus indica* (Colebr. Ex. Camb) HK., *Juglens regia* L., *Pyrus phashia* Buch-Ham ex. D. Don. Among the shrubs, *Colqunonia coccinea* Wall, *Berberis aristata* D. C., *Caragana vessicolor* (Wall) Benth and *Cotoneaster microphyllus* Wall ex. Lindl. were present. The ground vegetation was mainly dominated by *Apluda mutica* L., *Sporoplus* sp., *Geranium nepalense* SW., *Origanum vulgare* and *Malva verticillata* L.

Site-3 (Tolma): This North-Western part of Nanda Devi Biosphere Reserve represents an alpine Coniferous forest. A total of 45 species of plants, which included 11 species of trees, 11 species of shrubs and 23 species of herbs, were recorded from this study site durin 1998-2001. Dominant species of trees, shrubs and herbs included *Cupressus torolosa* D. Doon., *Cedrus deodara* (Roxb) Loud, *Pinus wallichina* Jacks, *Artenisia nilagrica* (CL) Pamp, *Berberis aristata* D. C., *Arundinaria spathiflora* Trin, *Rubus biflorus* Buch-Ham ex. Sm. and *Colqunonia coccinea* Wall.

Among the ground vegetation, *Thalictrum pauciflorum* Royle, *Sporoplus* sp. and *Apluda mutica* L.

Site-4 (Dunagiri): A total of 48 species of plants (trees-7, shrubs-18 and herbs-23) were recorded from this site. Dunagiri represents a moist sub alpine shrub forest dominated by *Betula utilis* D. Don, *Pinus wallichiana* Jacks, *Picea smithiana* (Wall) Boiss, *Taxus baccata* L. sub sp. and *Lyonia ovalifolia* (Wall) Drude. Besides trees, the dominant species of shrubs and herbs recorded were *Berberis asitica* D. C., *Arundinaria spathiflora* Trin, *Arundinaria falcata* Nees, *Hypericum uralum* Buch-Ham ex. D. Don, *Urtica dioica* L., *Salvia campanulata* L., *Thalictrum panciflorum* Royle, *Viburnum cotinifolicem*, *Fragaria nubicola* Lindl. ex. Lacaita, *Euphrasia himalayica* HK.F., *Anaphalis contorta* (Sins.) Cl., *Polygonum polysta* Chyum Wall and *Anaphalis triplinensis* (Sims.) Cl.

Taxonomic Composition of Different Insect Orders

The detailed taxonomic composition of different insect orders recorded from all the four study sites during the study period.

Order Lepidoptera : Lepidoptera was the most dominant order in the study area and was represented by 1764 individuals belonging to 18 species and 5 families during the study period 1998-2001. On the basis of number of identified species Pieridae was the most dominant family of this order with 7 species, followed by Nymphalidae (5), Satyridae (3), Lycaenidae (2) and Danidae (1).

Pieridae was the most dominant family, represented by 827 individuals during 1998-2001, and constituted 46.88% of total collected Lepidoptera. *Pieris canidia indica* Sparr. was the most dominant species of this family that constituted 56.60% of total of this family, followed by *Colias electro fieldi* Mensteris (16.57%), *Aporia agathon Caphisa* Moore (13.90%), *Gonopteryx rhamni nepalensis* Debl. (4.47%) and *Delias belladona belladona* (Gray) (2.42%). Satyridae was the second dominant family of this order constituting 23.07% of the total collected Lepido-pterans. *Aulocera swaha swaha*

Koll. was the dominant species of this family which constituted 51.35% of this family, followed by *Ypthima* sp. (29.73%) and *Parage schakara* Koll. (18.92). Nymphalidae constituted 15.70% of the total collected Lepidopterans during 1998-2001. *Vansessa caschmirensis* Fru. was the most dominant species of this family and constituted 42.69% of total individuals of this family, followed by *Neptis yerburyi* (But.) (28.52%), *Pyramis cardui cardui* (But.) (14.45%) and *Argynmis lathonia issea* Debl. (12.27%). Lycaenidae was represented by 2 species and constituted 13.94% of total Lepidopterans individuals collected. *Heodes pavana* (Koll.) was the dominant species of this family constituted 58.13% of the total number, followed by *Heliophorus* sp. (41.87%). Danidae was represented by *Dannus* sp., which constituted 0.47% of the total individuals of Lepdioptera.

Order Hymenoptera : Hymenoptera, the second most dominant order in the study area was represented by 1471 individuals belonging to 15 species and 7 families during the study period. On the basis of number of identified species Apidae was the most dominant family of this order with 5 species, followed by Scolidae (3), Vespidae and Ichneu-monidae (2 each), Pomplidae, Sphecidae and Eumenidae (1 each).

Family Apidae constituted 43.64% of total collected Hymenopteran individuals. This family was dominated by *Bombus* sp., which constituted 35.67% of total individuals of this family, followed by *Apis laborosia* Smith (25.39%), *Anthophora* sp. (25.59%), *Crocisa ramosa* (Lepel) (10.43%) and *Coeloxys* sp. (5.92%). Vespidae was the second dominant family of this order, which constituted 23.99% of the total collected Hymenopterans during the study period. *Vespa velutina auraria* Smith was the dominant species of this family which constituted 62.64% of total individuals of this family, followed by *Polistes maculipennis* (Saum) (29.73%). Family Ichneumonidae was represented by 2 species and constituted 11.09% of the total collected Hymenopterans during 1998-2001. *Ichneumon species and Ophion species* constituted 63.19% and 36.81% of this family respectively. Family Scolidae constituted 10.33% of total Hymenopteran individuals collected during the study period. *Campsomeris asiatica himalaya* Bar. was the most dominant species of this family constituting 46.05% of the total number of this family, followed by *Scolia venusta* (Smith) (28.29%), *Elias* sp. (25.66%). Family Sphecidae was represented by *Ammophila punctata* (Smith) which constituted 6.92% of the total Hymenopteran individuals. Family Pomplidae was represented by *Salius flavans* Fabr. which constituted 3.38% of the total Hymenopteran individuals. Family Eumenidae was represented by *Eumenes punctata* (Saussure) which Constituted 0.54% of the total Hymenopteran individuals.

Order Coleoptera : Order Orthoptera was represented by 1267 individuals belonging to 14 species and 2 families during the study period. On the basis of number of identified species Acrididae was the most dominant family of this order with 8 species followed by family Tettigonidae with 6 species.

Acrididae constituted 87.33% of the total collected Orthopterans during the study period. *Xenocatantops karnyi* Kirby was the dominant species of this family which constituted 17.85% of total individuals, followed by *Aulacobthrus leutipus* Walk. (17.04%), *Oedipoda himalayana* (Walk.) (15.78%), *Oedipoda* sp. (14.34%), *Chorthippus* sp. (13.98%), *Paraconophyma scabra* (Walk.) (12.35), *Spathosternum pr. prasniferum* (Walk.) (4.87%) and *Gastrimarqus transversus* (Thun.) (3.79%). Tettigonidae was represented by 158 individuals belonging to 6 species which constituted 12.47% of the total collected Orthopterans. This family was mainly dominated by *Mecapoda* sp. which constituted 25.95% of total of this family, followed by *Conocephalus maculatus* (Le Glue) (20.25%), *Phaneroptera gracilis* (Walk.) (17.09%), *Himmertula kinneri* (Uvarov) (13.29%), *Elimae* sp. (13.29%) and *Letana linearis* Walk. (8.07%).

Order Coleopetra: Order Coleoptera was represented by 14 species belonging to 6 families during the study period 1998-2001 and data are presented. On the basis of number of identified species Scrabidae and Chrysomelidae were the most dominant families represented by 4 species each followed by Meloidae and Coccinellidae (2 each), Elateridae and Curculonidae (1 each).

Scarabaeidae was the most dominant family of this order, which constituted 35.30% of total collected Coleopteran individuals. *Pretaetia neglecta* (Hope) was the most dominant species of this family which constituted 62.02% of total individuals of this family, followed by *Jumnous roylei* (Hope) (14.52%), *Sisyphus hirtus* Wied (12.85%) and *Anamola* sp. (10.61%). Chrysomelidae was the second dominant family of this order constituting 30.58% of the total collected Coleopterans during the study period. *Altica himensis* (Shukla) was the most dominant species of this family which constituted 59.03% of total number of individuals of this family, followed by *Cassida* sp. (23.87%), *Paridea* sp. (12.58%) and *Mimastra* sp. (4.52%). Coccinellidae was represented by 2 species and constituted 12.23% of total collected Coleopterans. *Coccinella septumpunctata* (L.) was the dominant species of this family, which constituted 78.40% followed by *Halyzia sanscrita* Muls (21.60%). Elateridae was represented by *Agrypnus* sp. which constituted 11.24% of total collected Coleopterans during the study period. Family Meloidae constituted 6.31% of all the Coleopterans. This family represented by the 2 species, *viz.*, *Mylabris cichonni* (L.) and *Meloe violaceous* (Mars) during the study period. Family Curcullonidae was also represented by only one species *Sympiezomias cretaceons* Fst. with very few number of individuals constituting 4.25% all the Coleopterans.

Order Odonata : Order Odonata was represented by 11 species belonging to three families. On the basis of number of identified species, Libellulidae was the most dominant family of this order with 8 species, followed by Ashinidae (2) and Cordulidae (1).

Family Libellulidae constituted 60.64% of total Odonates collected. *Crocothemis servilia servilia* (Drury) was the most dominant species of this family, which constituted 16.41% of total individuals of this family, followed by *Sympetrum commixtum* Fabr. (15.26%), *Orthretrum taeniolatum* Sch. (14.12%), *Orthretrum glaucum* Branr.

(13.36%), *Orthretrum pruinosum* neglectum Rmb. (11.45%), *Palpopleura sexmaculata sexmaculata* Fabr. (11.06%), *Pantala flavascens* Fabr. (9.54%) and *Orthetrum sabina sabina* Drury. (8.79%). Family Aeschnidae constituted 28.47% of the all Odonates. *Annax imaculifron* R. was the dominant species of this family, which constituted 53.66% of total of this family, followed by *Annax nigrofaciatus nigrolineatus* Fraser. (46.34%). Family Cordulidae was represented by *Macromia moorei* Sleys which constituted 10.88% of total collected Odonates.

Order Dipetra : Order Diptera was represented by 852 individuals belonging to 11 species and 6 families during the study period. On the basis of number of identified species Asilidae and Syrphidae werer the most dominant families of order Diptera represented by 3 species each, followed by Tabaenidae (2), Bombylidae and Tipulidae (1 each).

Asilidae was the most dominant family of this order, which constituted 33.34% of total collected Dipterans. *Machimus* sp. was the most dominant species of this family which constituted 37.62% of total individuals of this family, followed by *Stenopogou oldroydi* (Joseph and Pauri) (35.91%) and *Cryptopogon* sp. (26.41%). Family Syrphidae was the second dominant family of this order constituting 27.46% of the total collected Dipterans during the study period. *Syrphus fulvifacies* Brunetti was the most dominant species of this family which constituted 69.66% of total number of this family, followed by *Atylotus* sp. (21.29%) and *Sphaerophoria* sp. (8.55%). Tabaenidae constituted 19.07% of total collected Diptearns. *Hybomitra* sp. was the dominant species of this family, which constituted 61.12% of total number of individuals of this family, followed by *Philoche* sp. (38.88%). Family Tachnidae was represented by *Servilia* sp. constituting 7.86% of all collected Dipterans during the study period. Bombylidae and Bombylidae were also represented by single species each *viz., Bombylieus major* (L.) constituting 6.34% and *Tipula* sp. 5.99% of total collected Dipterans, respectively.

Order Hemiptera: Order Hemiptera was represented

by 8 species belonging to 4 families. On the basis of number of identified species Pentatometidae was the most dominant family of this order with 3 species, followed by Coreidae (3), Reduridae (1) and Cicadellidae (1).

On the basis of number of individuals collected from the study area, during 1998-2001, Family Reduridae was the most dominant family with a single species *Rhinocoris renteri* Dist. which constituted 41.46% of total collected Hemipterans. Pentatometidae was the second most dominant family, which constituted 29.05% of all Hemipterans. *Carpoeoris pallidus* Dalls was the dominant species of this family, which constituted 31.16% while *Delyeoris baccarum constituted* 35.65%. Family Coreidae constituted 17.22% of total collected Hemipterans. *Homeocrus* sp. was the dominant species of this family constituting 44.06% of total of this family, followed by *Anoplocnemis phasina* Fabr. (38.99%) and *Cletus punctuatus* Wetward (16.95%). Family Cicadidae was represented by the single species, *Pycna repanda* Linn., which constituted 12.27% of total collected Hemipterans.

DENSITY AND BIOMASS OF INSECTS

The maximum and minimum densities varied from 3.66/ha.(16/12/98) to 66.33/ha.(14/08/99) in Siite-1 **(Raini)** during 1998-1999 and from 5.33 /ha. (15/12/99) to 73.66 /ha. (14/07/2000) during second year of study, 1999-2000, while from 5/ha (18/12/2000) to 42/ha (18/04/2001) during 2000-2001.

In the Site-2 (Lata) density varied from 1.66 /ha. (17/02/98) to 63.66 /ha. (15/02/99) during 1998-1999, while from 2.33/ha. (14/02/2000) to 58.33 /ha. (15/07/2000) during the second year of study 1999-2001 and 1.00 /ha (16/02/2001) to 2.33 /ha (19/04/2001) during the third year of study period.

In the Site-3 (Tolma) density varied from 1.00 /ha. (18/12/98) to 93 /ha. (16/08/99) during 1998-1999, while from 2.66 /ha. (17/12/2000) to 56.33 /ha. (18/06/2000) during 1999-2001 and 2.00 /ha (17/02/2001) to 28 /ha (21/04/2001) during the study period 2000-2001.

In the Site-4 (Dunagiri) density varied from 8.00 /ha. (16/02/98) to 56.00 /ha. (17/08/99) during 1998-1999, while from 1.00 /ha. (18/11/1999) to 50.33 /ha. (17/09/2000) during 1999-2001 and 2 /ha (18/02/2001) to 18.33 (22/04/2001) during 2000-2001.

In the present study higher insect densities were recorded during the rainy season, when temperature and humidity remain best suitable optimum range and the food plants (Herbs, Shrubs, Grasses) were available in plenty, while low insects density were recorded during winter season which may be attributed to extreme climatic conditions, *viz.*, very low atmospheric temperature, high velocity of wind and heavy snow fall in the study site (Western Part of Nanda Devi Biosphere Reserve). One region for the low number of insects recorded during the winter season may be due to our inability to visit the study site in early winters due to extremely unfavourable weather conditions. However, the presence and absence of species in any area depends on a variety of other factors also including the availability of food plants/material and anthropogenic activities etc. Studies conducted so far on entomofuana of Western Part of Nanda Devi Biosphere Reserve show a rich diversity of this group in the area.

The higher densities of insects were recorded during the month of August 1999 and July 2001 in Site-1 **(Raini).** It was due to higher number of *Odipoda himalayana* Walk. (Orthoptera: Acrididae) and *Anthophora* sp. (Hymenoptera: Apidae) and maximum availability of insect food plants and emergence of Acrided instar.

In Site-2 (Lata) higher values of insect densities were recorded during the month of August 1999 and July 2001. It was because of higher number of *Xenocatantops karnyi* Kirby (Orthoptera : Acrididae) and *Altica himensis* Shukla (Coleoptera : Chrysomellidae). This Chrysomedllid (Flea beetle) feeds only on *Rumux hestatus* pants sp., which is available in plenty during this period.

In Site-3 (Tolma) higher insect densities were also recorded during rainy season. It was due to maximum number of *Rhinocoris reuteri* Dble (Reduridae : Hemiptera). Clustes of this species collected from the leaves of *Placoranthus coestea* plant species. Rainy season is best suitable for the blooming of this plant species.

In Site-4 (**Dunagiri**) maximum densities were recorded during the month of Aug. and Sep. It was because of higher number of butterfly sp., *Parage schakara* Koll. (Sytridae : Lepidoptera) and *Vanessa indica* (Nymphalidae : Lepidoptear).

Biomass : The data on variation in biomass (mg/ha.) and density (/ha.) recorded during the first year of study period 1998-1999 are presented. The total biomass of insects varied from 4135.13 mg/ha. (14/08/99) to 167.1 mg/ha. (13/02/99) in Site-1 (**Raini**), from 3620.31 mg/ha. (15/08/99) to 61.13 mg/ha. (17/12/98) in Site-2 (**Lata),** from 3929.66 mg/ha. (16/08/99) to 29.9 mg/ha. (18/12/98) in Site-3 (**Tolma**), while from 3141.46 mg/ha. (17/08/99) to 178.4 mg/ha. (16/02/99) in Site-4 **(Dunagiri).**

The total biomass of insects varied from 3890.20 mg/ha. (14/09/2000) to 200.63 mg/ha. (15/03/2000) in Site-1 (Raini), from 3305.2 mg/ha. (16/08/2000) to 32.4.86 mg/ha. (14/02/2000) in Site-2 (Lata), from 3600.2 mg/ha. (17/08/2000) to 69.53 mg/ha. (17/12/99) in Site-3 (Tolma), and from 1999.86 mg/ha. (1709/2000) to 41.6 mg/ha. (13/02/2000) in Site-4 (Dunagiri). During 2000-2001 biomass varied from 210.33 mg/ha (16/03/2001) to 1725.07 mg/ha (18/04/2001) in Site-1 (Raini), from 32.33 mg/ha (16/02/2001) to 1525.00 mg/ha (19/04/2001) in Site-2 (Lata), from 76.33 mg/ha (17/02/2001) to 1244.93 mg/ha (19/03/2001) in Site-3 (Tolma) and from 103.33 mg/ha (18/02/2001) to 1192.63 mg/ha (22/04/2001) in Site-4 (Dunagiri).

The higher values of densities were recorded during rainy season, while the maximum biomass was also generally recorded in the rainy season or early winters. The reason for the higher densities during rainy season may be emergence of instars of insects of different insect groups, while on late rainy season the number of adult with increased biomass.

Trophic Level Composition of Insects

Trophic level composition of insects on the basis of number of individuals collected and their per cent contribution to the total population during 1998-2001, while trophic level composition of different insect orders in terms of number of species collected and their per cent contribution to total population during 1998-2001.

It is a well-known fact that Herbivores are the dominant constituents in all the habitats, in terms of number of individuals and species collected from any ecosystem. On the basis of number of individuals, Herbivores (53.63%) constituted the maximum of all the insects collected during 1998-1999, followed by Predators (42.37%) and Saprophagous (4.03%). During 1999-2001 Herbivores constituted 60.01% of the total collected individuals, followed by Predators (34.48%) and Saprophagous (5.51%).

Herbivores: A total of 4225 individuals of the Herbivorrous species of different insects orders were collected during the study period 1998-2001, which included Lepidoptera 18 species and 1764 individuals, followed by Orthoptera 14 species and 1267 individuals, Coleoptera (Chrysomelidae, Curculionidae and partially Coccinellidae) 6 species and 380 individuals, Hymenoptera (Apidae) 5 species and 642 individuals and Hemiptera (Cicadidae, Coreidae) 4 species and 202 individual.

Predators: A total of 2872 individuals of Predator insects were collected during the study period, which included, Diptera 11 species and 852 individuals, followed by Odonata 11 species and 432 individuals, Hymenoptera (Vespidae, Ichenumonidae, Sphecidae, Pomplidae, Eumenidae) 10 species and 839 individuals, Hemiptera (Pentatometidae, Reduridae) 4 species and 483 individuals, Coleoptera (Meloidae, Elaterida, Coccinellidae) 4 species and 266 individuals.

Saprophages: A small number of Saprophagous insects were which included 4 species and 358 individuals of order Coleoptera and family Scarabacidae during study period 1998-2001.

ENERGY BUDGET

The biomass, consumption and egesta were comparatively higher in females than males. The biomass in males ranged from 23.65 (3rd instar) to 56.12 (adult) mg insect-1 day-1 while in female it ranged between 28.35 (3rd instar) to 104.30 (adult) mg insect-1 day-1. The average rate of consumption in males ranged from 14.78 to 30.92 mg insect-1 day-1 while in females it ranged from 15.84 to 40.55 mg insect-1 day-1. Male grasshoppers had a slightly higher assimilation rate than females and it ranged between 9.23 to 17.84 mg insect-1 day-1 and 6.79 to 16.52 mg insect-1 day-1 respectively. Females had higher tissue growth than males. In males it ranged from 1.58 to 3.98 mg insect-1 day-1 while in females it ranged between 3.02 to 7.88 mg insect-1 day-1. Matsumoto, (1971) and Vats and Kaushal, (1981) reported that the rate of consumption and egestion were higher in females than males.

Ecological efficiency is defined as a ratio of any two parameters of energy flow in or between the trophic levels of natural community, in or between population or organisms (Odum, 1959). The apparent digestibility was higher in 3rd nymphal instars of males and 3rd and 4th instars of females. The decline in digestibility from 5th instar to adult may have been due to the fact younger stages were fed on soft and more succulent tender leaves, whereas the adults were fed on leaves, which were more fibrous. The males are more efficient in assimilating the consumed food.

The ECD is a measure of efficiency with which absorbed food material is used in promoting the growth. This parameters significantly increased from 3rd nymphal instar to adult in both the sexes and females had higher values than males. The efficiency of conversion of ingested food (ECI) also increased with development and females were having higher value than males. Hussian and Pfadt, (1976) studied food utilization across development stages of big headed grasshopper, *Alucara elliotti* Thomas and reported that the ingestion of food ranged from 27.8 to 215.3 mg insect-1 day-1 in males and from 26.2 to 411.8 mg insect-1 day-1 in females, suggesting a markedly grater intake of food compared to present investigation. This difference is reasonable given that the values for ECD ranged between 6 to 26% in males and 4 to 39% in females of *A. elliotti* Thomas, indicating much poor conversion efficiency.

The utilization rates and assimilation efficiencies we measured in the present study fall in the range of other reported grasshopper species, (Smelly, 1960; Wiegert, 1965; Gyllenberg, 1969; Van Hook, 1971; Duke and Crossley, 1975; Singhal, *et.al.*,1976; White, 1978; Delvi and Pandian, 1979; Vats and Mittal, 1983; Kaushal and Vats, 1984; Kohler, *et. al.,* 1987 and Kaushal and Joshi, 1991). These finding suggest that *Xenocatantops karnyi* K. females are significantly larger than males and consume less biomass per unit of body weight. Female grasshoppers have a significantly higher tissue growth than males. Assimilation and tissue growth were positively related to the amount of food consumed. With increase in age and biomass, apparent digestibility declined but ECD & ECI increased.

Endangered Fauna: Apart from our studies on insect diversity in the selected sites in NDBR, literature surveyed on the reserve shows presence of 18 mammals and nearly 200 birds in the area. Of these, the following species of mammals and birds belong to the endangered catagories:

Mammals: 1. Musk deer 2. Himalayan tahr 3. Bharal 4. Serow 5. Black bear 6. Brown bear 7. Snow leopard.

Birds: 1. Black eagle 2. Bearded vulture 3. Golden eagle 4. Him snow cock 5. Koklas pheasant 6. Monal pheasant 7. Steppe eagle 8. Western tragopan.

Nanda devi Biosphere Reserve is thus rich in biological diversity and enhabits a large number of rare and endangered species of flora and fauna and some of which are endemic to this area.

6

Aquatic Resources and Fish Biodiversity

The Himalayan region is usually regarded as a cold water regime, though this is not fully so. But still as compared to the Indo-Gangetic Plains and rest of the Indian peninsular region, the Himalayan waters are relatively colder. Apart from the thermal factor, the geo-topography of whole of the mountain region is highly varied and hostile, with very fast turbulence to very narrow deep caved gorges in one hand to highly bouldered rocky substratum to soft sandy bottom. On the basis of elevation and temperature regime the Himalayan streams are classified in three principal types by Jhingaran and Sehgal (1978) and Sehgal (1983). These water bodies usually have higher dissolved oxygen contents, high transparency, very low biochemical and chemical oxygen demands and relatively a low productivity.

A high velocity of water current is a major constraint in the lower primary productivity of the aquatic bodies of this region. In the recent years interest to know the general eco-biological characteristics of the Himalayan streams. It has increased and adequate information is available about a number of water bodies from this region (Aunder *at. al.*, 1978, Joshi, Sehgal and Sunder, 1978; Nautiyal 1986; Joshi

1988,a, b, Joshi *et. al.*, 1992, a, b; Joshi *et. al.*, 1993, a, b; Agarwal and Singh, 1993, Nautiyal and Nautiyal 1995; Nautiyal *et. al.*, 1996; Joshi and Kathait 1998; Kishore *et. al.*, 1998; Joshi and Singh 1999 and Bhatt *et. al.*, 2000). However, the major aquatic network of the Himalayan belt is still virgin and offers a wide scope, to explore the hydro-biological characteristics of various water bodies.

The whole of the Himalayan belt towards Indian side, that is south of the Himalayas is well endowed with a number of major rivers having wide spread catchment areas. Sehgal (1992) has enlisted 15 major rivers, 12 high altitude lakes, 10 low altitude lakes and 03 reservoir, spread between greater Himalayas and lesser Himalayas and its foothills. The hydro biological or the physico-chemical characteristics of many of these water bodies have been partially worked out as briefly included in the fore going description. But most of the eco-biological reports on these aquatic resources are repeatedly site/location/region specific and hardly one or two are holistic in their approach (Joshi, 1993). Apart from being micro-regional, the ambient environmental conditions are far from routinely seasonal, on account of number of anthropogenic activities, which have reached to the root of these various Himalayan rivers or up to the peak of the Himalayan mountains. As a result there are wide fluctuations and abnormal variations in all sorts of ecosystems around us; the Himalayan aquatic eco-system is no exception. For example there is still no agreement among few of the Indian limnologists that what criterion should be applied in describing the various types of water bodies spread in this region. This is mainly due to two main reasons: first there are highly discernible conspicuous differences in the geographical placement of these water bodies. These differences are related mainly to altitude, topography of the region, river beds, gradients, types of the mountain on one hand and secondly the related physico-chemical characteristics like temperature, transparency, turbidity, pH, depth, river span and water velocity which are different from each other. All these parameters cumulatively exert a very unique influence on the primary productivity of a given system, which ultimately becomes a deterministic characteristic on its total biotic community (Joshi, 1998).

Despite a variable dynamism, each system tries to attain sort of a stable predictable behavioural pattern. And this tendency of an eco-system creates various types of adaptive divergences, leading to species diversity. Now all these abiotic and the biotic components make a system quite specific. These characteristics have been used by few authors (Zutshi and Khan, 1978; Sehgal, 1988; Nautiyal and Nautiyal, 1995 and Joshi *et. al.*, 1978) in suggesting classifications of Kashmir valley lakes and Himalayan rivers. This specificity is not an entire one, but is segmented in various regions of the same water body (Sehgal, 1992; Joshi, 1993 and 1998, Kishore *et. al.*, 1998; Nautiyal and Nautiyal, 1995 and Singh and Kumar, 2000).

Even the same river can be classified in to several altitudinal zones on the basis of just three parameters *viz.*, Altitude, temperature and dissolved oxygen contents in the water. And this does not include the short-term ambient influences of minor tributaries, besides the pollutional impacts of myriad types, which are soon mitigated on account of self-rejuvenating characteristics of these aquatic ecosystems, unless there is no recurrence of any hostile feeder stream. The whole of the Bhagirathi-Ganga system is a very good example of it, reflecting a high rejuvenating capacity in the uplands, which gets diluted once it enters the Indo-Gangetic plains and is almost totally lost by the time Ganga crosses the Kanpur zone.

Similarly the most of the lacusterine systems of up land valleys have lost their originality, productivity and are fast getting eutrophicated on account of various types of the effluents being discharged in to them. As a result most of these lotic as well as lentic water bodies of the Himalayan region are fast loosing their primary productivity on one hand and there are observable break downs in the complicated food chains/webs with in each system, independent of each other, for similar systems, with in the same geographical habitat or else where. All these minor casual faults or variations ultimately, cumulatively blow up in to definite patters, changing the niche dynamics and there by niche occupancy of the biota, in the long food chain affecting the bio-diversity of micro or macro-community component/ participant. This what is actually happening in many mountain pockets. This is amply reflected in the species dynamics or the bio-diversity parameters of these mountain aquatic bodies.

THE STATUS OF FISH FAUNA OF THE HIMALAYAN REGION

Mother nature has been quite benevolent to our Indian sub-continent in equipping it with most varied zoogeographical and climatological zones, spread through the length and breadth of this country. This has consequently resulted in equally most varied biospheric regions, harboring myriad types of terrestrial and aquatic habitats, further sub-divided in innumerable, microhabitats and highly specific ecological niches. Such abiotic diversity is further manifested by mother Nature in equally one of the richest biodiversity within the geo-political boundaries of India, falling under the Oriental zoo-geographical region. The endemic fish fauna of Himalayan region finds its record from our most ancient Vedic era. According to Hora (1951) the most famous Mahseer fish species of *Tor putitora* find its mention under the name of Mahasalka , most probably on account of its large sized body scales. However, as for the recent historical past it was most probably Hamilton (1822), who for the first time documented a number of hill stream fishes from the sub Himalayan region, followed by McClelland (1835), who described the fishes from the Kumaon region of the Himalayas. During the same period Hechel (1838) documented the presence of about 15 species of fresh water fishes from the Jhelum valley of the Kashmir, based on the field collection of Kari Alexander Anslem Von Hugel, during his surveys (1931-1936). Hugel is reported to have deposited his collection samples in the Museum of Natural History in

Vienna, Austria. Where Jacob Heckal was working as an Ishthyologist. These authors are followed by Gunther (1861) and Day (1878-79), who described a record number of fishes from the Himalayan mountain region.

During the 20th century, work on various aspects of Himalayan mountain fish fauna were carried out by a number of authors (Hora, 1932, a,b,c, 1940, 1952, 1955; Hutchinson; Menon 1949, 1954, 1962, 1992; Mishra 1962; Das 1965; Sehgal 1959, 1972, 1974, a,b,c, 1990, 1991, 1992; Joshi, Sehgal and Sunder 1978; Sehgal *et al.,* 1988; Pant 1970; Badola and Pant 1973; Badola and Singh 1977a,b; Jhingaran and Sehgal 1987; Joshi 1994, 1998). Most of these authors have described fish fauna of western and north central Himalayan states.

In fact the Himalayan fish fauna includes even those fishes too, which are found in the Nepal part of the Himalayas. Similarly the north-eastern states of India *viz.*, Assam, Manipur, Sikkim, Arunachal etc., are also part of the Himalayan aquatic system. However, its published literature is not available to the authors of this book, till now. Hence, this chapter primarily enlists the distribution of fishes from the states of Jammu and Kashmir, Himachal Pradesh, and Uttaranchal . It is mainly on account of the fact that these states harbor relatively, commercially more important fishes than rest of the Himalayan region. Further, the fish fauna of the whole Himalayan belt is by and large almost common, but for specific endemic diversity.

Till now presence of 256 species of fresh water teleosts, belonging to 62 genera, 11 sub families, 12 families and 05 orders have been reported from various aquatic resources of the western to north-central Himalayan region, during almost last two centuries of fish diversity and taxonomic surveys–till date, by the various authors and groups.

It will be interesting to evaluate that what is the real present day status of fish diversity in the Himalayan mountain region. From the existing literature three points emerge: (*a*) still many remote areas are to be explored to find out the species diversity, (*b*) in view of reported divergence in speciation for certain species like *Schizothorax, Puntius, Garra, Glyptosternum, and Noemachilus* there are chances that correct taxonomic identification may show synonimity, and (*c*) many species are already on the verge of extinction from this region.

A critical analysis points out that out of 256 species enlisted here as Himalayan fish fauna–(for the prescribed region) about 93 species fall under Threatened group. The threatened status includes 22 vulnerable species, 16 intermediate species, 48 rare species and 07 Endangered species (for the Himalayan region, perhaps ?) as described by a few earlier workers of the subject (Menon 1974, Tilak and Hussain 1977, and Sehgal 1992). It is quite obvious that many species are highly niche specific and endemic. The typical endemism simply means the organism of the given habitat or area would be critically highly vulnerable to slightest unfavorable variations in its ambient environment. And as we all known that under the present global scenario and with an attitude of – who cares for the environment, we have severely exposed our aquatic environment to several types of anthropogenic alterations. These alteration pose myriad types of physical (*viz.*, mid stream construction activities, embankment erosions), chemical (use of detergent, chemical fertilizers, pesticides) and biological (introduction of new species exotic or extra territorial ones, introduction or removal or extinction of other community components) challenges to some very micro-habitat oriented and adapted endemic organisms. Absence of even one or two organisms in the long inter-connected food web in any given system would snow ball to grave biological threats at one or other level, and Himalayan ecology, as it stands today is most vulnerable to such conditions, right from the top of say Everest to the base line spots like Hardwar, Haldwani and Jammu to Meghalaya.

Fishery Scenario in Himalayan Region

The present day fishery scenario in Himalayan region can be said almost red (alert) to blackish black (bleak, too), rather being rosy pink. Nearly similar observations have been made by Joshi *et al.,* (1978), for the western to north central Himalayan fishery, while describing fishery resources of the Jammu region. These authors have mentioned that *Oreinus plagiostomus* constitutes about 29%, and *Barrilius bendelisis* about 28% (in trout streams), while *Tor putitora* constitutes about 30% (in the mahseer streams) highest for the region. According to Singh *et. al.,* (1993) six common species, which contribute to the real fishery to the Uttaranchal, are *Oreinus richardsonii, Tor putitora, Labeo dero, Barilius bendelisis, Garra gotvla gotyla and Crossocheilus latius latius*. Our own field surveys show that in the Garhwal Himalayan region *Schizothorax sps*., and *Tor sps*. contribute more than 60-70% (of the total fish haul), followed by *Barilius* sps and *Glyptothorax* sps. Joshi (1993) have reported about 47%, 18% and 16% of *Schizothorax, Tor* and *Glptothorax* species in the random surveys around Tehri.

A gradual decline in the length weight frequency of the fish catch/ haul for the Garhwal region is also apparent. There is increasingly greater exploitation of smaller sized fishes at all levels. In the colder mountain regime, it is basically *Schizothorax* sps, which predominates other, while at lower mountain altitude or among the spring fed rivers and streams it is *Tor* sps. Which contributes maximum, at single species consideration. However, over the years it is almost the juvenile to quite immature age groups of these species, which are exploited. In our own observations we found fish weighing about 6-7 kg only, around Srinagar (Joshi, 1993) and that a general trend in fall of length and weight range of fish hauled between Tehri - Uttarkashi and Srinagar–Rishikesh is quite conspicuous.

As far mahseer, the major fish of the middle to lower Himalayan region is concerned, there is a general decline through the belt, ranging a fall between 15 to as high as 63% for the Kumaun lakes and the Gobindsagar reservoir. This trend only shows that increasingly more and more amount of immature fishes are being hauled. Certainly this would lead to further decline in fish productivity of the region, for want of appropriate number of new recruting to spawner in these streams, in near future.

CAUSES OF FISH DECLINE

This part does not require any special elaboration on the question of causes of decline. If a single word can be selected to reply it absolutely then the answer is obviously. The MAN, himself, is the only and sole reason of such a rapid decline of quality fish fauna and in quantum, besides, in their diversity. However, after spoiling and reaching to the threatened level of over exploitation, we try to act as saviors. In view of our this role following major reasons are attributed to the general decline:

I. An over all degradation of ambient microhabitat of fishes at all stages of their life cycle.

II. Over exploitation of our resources at all levels, irrespective of catch age group, reproductive period and season.

III. Increasing human activities of human beings with the aquatic environment on the name of recreation, tourism, and adventurism.

IV. Increasing anthropogenic encroachment ot aquatic areas for various developmental and agricultural activities.

V. Increase in deforestation, thereby fall in forest area, leading to enhanced soil erosion and siltation at various levels.

VI. Break down of aquatic food chains at various levels, on account of loss of one or other types of biotic components.

VII. Gradual decline of water level in smaller streams, on account of fast deforestation in the catchment areas of the uplands.

VIII. Use of traditional lethal to unnatural clandestine methods of poaching and fishing.

IX. An apathetic, neutral to careless attitude of responsible Govt. bodies towards conservation, protection and maintenance of fish health and their environment.

X. Rapid fall in the brooder population of fishes.

XI. Snow balling impacts of various sorts of pollutional causes and pollutants.

XII. Erractic and unpredictable changes in the climatological trends/patterns at global levels.

XIII. Appearance of fish epidemics at various levels.

XIV. Introduction of certain exotic varieties to the Himalayan streams or else where.

XV. Increasing eutrophication at certain levels, mainly on account of domestic effluents.

XVI. Developments of minor to major hydro-electric and irrigation projects, without appropriate majors towards fish movements, migration, feeding, spawning sand nursery grounds (In Uttaranchal alone there are about 20 minor to major such projects at various stages of development).

XVII. Fall in the biotic components at primary producer level in the aquatic ecosystems, due to various reasons.

XVIII. Fall in carrying capacity of various water bodies due to several anthropogenic and natural reasons.

XIX. Lack of our complete knowledge about various aspects of fish eco-biology and their environment.

XX. Lack of appropriate routine or advanced technology to mitigate various injurious impacts, due to financial or decision making constraints.

XXI. Lack of public awareness towards importance of maintenance of proper aquatic environment and fisheries potential in terms of nutritional and economic viability.

XXII. Lack of management expertise with regard to the routine fishery management, at various levels.

SYSTEMATIC LIST OF FISHES

Phylum	Vertebrata
Sub Phylum	Craniata

Super Class	Ganthostomata
Series	Pisces
Class	Teleostomi
Sub Class	Actinopterygii

ORDER CYPRINIFORMES

Family Cyprinidae **Sub Family Cyprininae**

1.	*Tor. putitora*	(Ham.)
2.	*T. tor*	(Ham.)
3.	*T. mosa*	(Ham.)
4.	*T. mosal mahnadicus*	(David)
5.	*T. khudree*	(Sykes)
6.	*T. proheneius*	(McCl)
7.	*T. cheilynoides*	(McCl)
8.	*Neolossochilius hexagonolepis*	(McCl)
9.	*N.qynaadensis*	(Day)
10.	*Oreinus richardsoni*	(Gray)
11.	*O. Kumaonensis*	(Menon)
12.	*Chagunius changunio*	(Ham.)
13.	Cirrhinus fulungee	(Sykes)
14.	*C.reba*	(Ham.)
15.	*Sehizothorax. curuifrons*	(Heckel)
16.	*S. esocinus*	(Heckel)
17.	*S. hugelli*	(Heckel)
18.	*S.longipinnis*	(Heckel)
19.	*S. micropogon*	(Heckel)
20.	*S. nasus*	(Heckel)
21.	*S. niger*	(Heckel)
22.	*S. macrophthalmus*	(Tarashima)
23.	*S. planifrons*	(Heckel)
24.	*S. raraensis*	(Tarashima)
25.	*S.kumaonensis*	(Menon)
26.	*S. sinuatus*	(Heckel)
27.	*S. plagiostomus*	(Heckel)
28.	*S. progastus*	(McCl)
29.	*S. labiatus*	(McCl)

30. *Diptychus maccelatus* (Steindachner)
31. *Lepidopygopsi. typus* (Raj)
32. *Schizopygopsis stoliczkae* (Steindachner)
33. *Gara gotyla gotyla* (Gray)
34. *G. annandalei* (Hora)
35. *G. bicornuta* (Rao)
36. *G. gravelyi* Anandale)
37. *G. hughi* (Silas)
38. *G. kempi* (Hora)
39. *G. Lamta* (Ham.)
40. *G. mcclellandi* (Jerdon)
41. *G. lissorhynchus* (McCl)
42. *G. mullya* (Sykes)
43. *G. naganensis* (Hora)
44. *Crossocheilus latius latius* (Heckel)
45. *C. latius diplocheilus* (Heckel)
46. *C.diplocheilus* (Heckel)
47. *Labeo labeo* (Ham.)
48. *L. bata* (Ham.)
49. *L. calbasu* (Ham.)
50. *L. pangusia* (Ham.)
51. *L. drycheilus* (McCl)
52. *L. boga* (Ham.)
53. *L. ginius* (Ham.)
54. *Puntis conchonius* (Ham.)
55. *P. ticto* (Ham.)
56. *P. arulius* (Jerdon)
57. *P. chola* (Ham.)
58. *P. dorsalis* (Jerdon)
59. *P. filamentosus* (Vale.)
60. *P. maheoda* (Vale.)
61. *P. sophore* (Ham.)
62. *P. waageni* (Day)
63. *P. bovanicus* (Day)
64. *P. jerdoni* (Day)
65. *P. carnaticus* (Jerdon)
66. *P. cauveriensis* (Hora)
67. *Bangana diplostoma* (Heckel)

68. *Hypophtalmichthys molotrix* (Vale.)
69. *Cteniohryngodon idella* (Vale.)
70. *Osteobrama cotio cunma* (Day)
71. *O. neilli* (Day)
72. *O.vigorsii* (Sykes)
73. *Osteochilus brevidoralis* (Day)
74. *O. nashii* (Day)
75. *Tinca tinca* (Linn.)

Sub Family Cultrinae

76. *Chela cashius* (Ham.)
77. *C. laubuca* (Ham.)
78. *C. bupis* (Day)
79. *Salmostoma phulo* (Ham.)
80. *S. untrachi* (Ham.)
81. *S. clupeoides* (Bloch)

Sub Family : Danioninae

82. *Barilius bendelisis* (Ham.)
83. *B. barna* (Ham.)
84. *B. canarensis* (Jerdon)
85. *B. shacra* (Ham.)
86. *B. tileo* (Ham.)
87. *B. vagra* (Ham.)
88. *B. barila* (Ham.)
89. *B. bota* (Ham.)
90. *Brachydanio rerio* (Ham.)
91. *Amblyphargngodn meletteies* (Vale.)

Sub Family Rasborinae

92. *Danio rerio* (Ham.)
93. *D. dario* *(McCl.)*
94. *D.* devario (Ham.)
95. *D. naganensis* (Chaudhari)
96. *D. neilgherriensis* (Day)
97. *D. acquipinnatus* (McCl)
98. *D. dangilla* (Ham.)
99. *Esomus barbatus* (Jerdon)

100. *E. danricus*	(Ham.)
101. *Rasbora bola*	(Ham.)
102. *R. guttatus*	(Day)
103. *R. rasbora*	(Ham.)
104. *R. daniconius*	(Ham.)

Sub Family : Schizothoracinae

105. *Ptychobarbus conirostris*	(Steindachner)
106. *Gymnocypris biswasi*	(Talwar)
107. *Scizothoraichthys curvifrons*	(Heckel)

Order Siluriformes	**Family Sisoridae**
108. *Glyptosternum pectinotterus*	(McCl)
109. *G. conuirostre conisrostre*	(Steidachner)
110. *G. trilineate*	(Blyth)
111. *G. cavia*	(Ham.)
112. *G. madraspatanum*	(Day)
113. *G. telchitta*	(Ham.)
114. *G. annandalei*	(Hora)
115. *G. ananmalaiensis*	(Silas)
116. *G. gracile*	(Gunther)
117. *G. indicus*	(Talwar)
118. *G. kashmirensis*	(Hora)
119. *G. platypogonoides*	(Bleeker)
120. *G. prashadi*	(Mukharjee)
121. *G. lonah*	(Sykes)
122. *G. stoliczkae*	(Steindachner)
123. *G. staiatus*	(McCl)
124. *G. dakpathari*	(Tilak and Hussain)
125. *G. garhwali*	(Tilak)
126. *G. alaknandi*	(Tilak)
127. *G. brevipinnis*	(Hora)
128. *G. trilineadus*	(Hora)
129. *Conta couta*	(Hora)
130. *Erethistes pussilus*	(Muler and Trochel)
131. *E. Montana Montana*	(Hora)

132. *E. Montana pipri* (Hora)
133. *Gagata cenia* (Ham.)
134. *G. gagata* (Ham.)
135. *G. sexualis* (Tilak)
136. *Laguvia ribeirot* (Hora)
137. *L. shavi* (Hora)
138. *L. kapuri* (Tilak and Hussain)
139. *L. asperus* (McCl)
140. *Sisor rhabdophorus* (Ham.)
141. *Pseudechenis sulcatus* (McCl.)
142. *Bagarius bagarius* (Ham.)

Family Schilbeidae

143. *Clupesome garua* (Ham.)
144. *C. Montana* (Ham.)

Sub Family Nemacheilinae

145. *Nemacheilus acuticephatus* (Hora)
146. *N. Anguilla* (Annandale)
147. *N. arafi* (Mirza and Banarescu)
148. *N. arunachalensis* (Menon)
149. *N. baluchiorum* (Zugmayer)
150. *N. beavani* (Gunther)
151. *N. botia* (Ham.)
152. *N. brevis* (Boulenger)
153. *N. brunneanus* (Ammandale)
154. *N. carletoni* (Fowler)
155. *N. cincticauda* (Blyth)
156. *N. corica* (Ham.)
157. *N. denisoni denisoni* (Day)
158. *N. densoni dayi* (Hora)
159. *N. devdevi* (Hora)
160. *N. doonensis* (Tilak and Hussain)
161. *N. elondatus* (Sen and Nalbant)
162. *N. evezardi* (Day)
163. *N. facimaculants* (Mirza and Nalbant)
164. *N. gangeticus* (Menon)
165. *N. guentheri* (Day)

166. *N. himachalensis* (Menon)
167. *N. horai* (Menon)
168. *N. kangjupkhulensis* (Day)
169. *N. keralensis* (Rita and Nalbant)
170. *N. Kessleri* (Gunther)
171. *N. kogaguensis* (Menon)
172. *N. kohatensis* (Mirza and Banareseu)
173. *N. labeosus* (Kottelat)
174. *N. lindbergi* (Banarseu and Mirza)
175. *N. monilis* (Hora)
176. *N. montanus* (McCl)
177. *N. moreh* (Sykes)
178. *N. multifasciatus* (Day)
179. *N. manupurensis* (Chaudhary)
180. *N.* nagaensis (Menon)
181. *N. nilgiriensis* (Menon)
182. *N. notostigma* (Bleeker)
183. *N. pakistanicus* (Mirza and Banareseu)
184. *N. pavonaceus* (McCl.)
185. *N. peguensis* (Hora)
186. *N. petrubanarescui* (Menon)
187. *N. parshadi* (Hora)
188. *N. reticulofasciatus* (Singh, Sen and Banar.)
189. *N. rivulicola* (Hora)
190. *N. rubidipinnis* (Blyth)
191. *N. rueppelli* (Sykes)
192. *N. rupicola* (McCl)
193. *N. sayana* (Ham.)
194. *N. scaturigina* (McCl.)
195. *N. semiarmatus* (Day)
196. *N. sijuensis* (Menon)
197. *N. sikmaiensis* (Hora)
198. *N. shanensis* (Hora)
199. *N. singhi* (Hora)
200. *N. striatus* (Menon)

201. *N. triangularis*	(Day)
202. *N. tuphthalmus*	(Gunther)
203. *N. vinciguerrae*	(Hora)
204. *N. zonalternaus*	(Blyth)
205. *Aborichthys elongates*	(Hora)
206. *A. garoensis*	(Hora)
207. *A. kempi*	(Chaudhari)
208. *A. tikaderi*	(Barman)
209. *Schistura pubjabensis*	(Hora)
210. *Triplophysa marmorata*	(Heckle)
211. *T. kashmirensis*	(Hora)

Sub Family Balitorinae

212. *Balitora brucei*	(Gray)
213. *B. mysorensis*	(Hora)
214. *Bhavania australis*	(Jerdon)
215. *Homaloptera bilineata*	(Blyth)
216. *H. Montana*	(Herre)
217. *H. rupicola*	(Prasad and Mukerji)
218. *Travancoria jonesi*	(Hora)

Family Cobitidae

Sub Family Botiinae

219. *Botia almorhae*	(Gray)
220. B. berbmorei	(Blyth)
221. B. birdi	(Chaudhari)
222. B. Dario	(Ham.)
223. B. striata	(Rao)
224. B. histrionica	(Blyth)
225. B. lohachata	(Chaudhari)
226. B. rostrata	(Gunther)

Sub Family Cobitinae

227. *Lepidocephalus guntea*	(Ham.)
228. *L. annanbalei*	(Chaudhari)
229. *L. berbmorei*	(Blyth)
230. *L. irrorata*	(Hora)
231. *L. menoni*	(Piuai and Yazdani)
232. *L. thermalis*	(Vale.)

233. *L.caudofurcatus* (Tilak & Hussain)
234. *Somileptes gongota* (Ham.)
235. *Pangipo pangio* (Ham.)
236. *P. longipinnis* (Menon)
237. *Neoencirrhichthys maydelli* (Banna & Nal.)

Family Amblyceitidae

238. *Amblyceps mangosis* (Ham.)
239. *A. laticees* (McCl.)

Family Bagridae

240. Mystus cavasius (Ham.)
241. *M. bleekeri* (Day)
242. *M. aor* (Ham.)
243. *M. seenghala* (Sykes)
244. *Batasio batasio* (Ham.)
245. *B. travancosia* (Hora & Law)

Family. Channidae

246. *Channa. gachua* (Ham.)
247. *C. orintalis* (Bloch & Schneider
248. *C. punctatus* (Bloch)

7

Case Study Insect Diversity in A Moist Deciduous Forest

Insects have adapted themselves over the evolutionary period of about 250-500 million years to the diverse environmental conditions. The dominance of insects may be attributed to the variability in their biological and ecological attributes. Insect ecologists have long tried to fathom out the mechanism of governing insect population densities, selection of niches by various species within their habitat. There are a wide variety of factors, which lead to the insects to select their habitat and different density dependent sources of mortality and key factors acting on the insect populations. The growing needs of human populations have led to the regular interference with a change in the insect habitats so much so that conflict between human and insects has become a vicious cycle of dominance of one over other. The study of insect biodiversity, therefore, represents a classic example of their adaptability to the wide range of environmental conditions. Out of the total known species of insects in the world about 6% are present in various habitats of India and many of them are endemic to this country.

Each forest has a distinct floristic composition, which varies in its species richness and the abundance of different species. Environmental variability in terms of climatic factors, soil resource, grazing by herbivores and, human interference are the critical factors, which regulate the spatial, and temporal pattern of species of an ecosystem. Keeping all these factors in mind a study was conducted in Rajaji National Park to assess the insect diversity, the role of various anthropogenic activities and also how the insects select micro-habitats to make survival in the fragmenting habitats. Following parameters of the forest ecosystem were studied:

(a) Study of abiotic factors which included temperature, humidity, soil pH, organic matter in soil and their seasonal fluctuations.
(b) Study of the floristic composition of the study sites selected in the Motichur Range of Rajaji National Park.
(c) Determination of population density, biomass and species diversity of insect fauna.
(d) Taxonomic composition and trophic components of insect.
(e) Effect of the insect fauna on vegetation and assessment of the damage.
(f) Identification of the stages causing damage and application of extract from the parts of certain plants like neem to see its effect in controlling the pest population out-break.
(g) Identification of various anthropogenic activities in the area, which have a bearing on the insect community.

SELECTION OF STUDY SITES IN MOTICHUR FOREST SANCTUARY

This study was carried out in Motichur Forest Sanctuary of Rajaji National Park during the years 1997-2000. This Park lies at foothills of Himalayas in Siwaliks. Survey of Rajaji National Park was conducted in order to select the study sites. Four study sites were selected in Motichur forest in four different blocks of the sanctuary. All the four sites differed from each other in vegetational composition and physical characteristics. The sites selected for the collection and study purposes were as under.

Site No. 1: It was a three-hectare piece of forest in the **Motichur Block of Sanctuary**. The study site was approximately 2.5 km form the forest approach road and was on the right hand side of the main river system of the sanctuary *i.e.*, the river song. The vegetation cover in this study site was not very dense. No ongoing disturbances were recorded from this study site during the study period. *Shorea robusta* Gaertn. and *Mellotus philippinensis* Mull-Arg., *Terminalia alata (Roxb)* and *T. bellerica* were the dominant species of trees in this site. The ground vegetation mainly comprised of *Cynodon dactylon, Desmodium laxiflorum, D. triangularie, Chrysopogon sp., Anelopteris prolifera, Leucas mollissima* and *Tephrosea perpurea.* This site was located at an altitude of 400 m from the mean sea level. Temperature at this site ranged between 14 ± 2 to 40 ± 2 C while humidity ranged between 19 to 89% during the study period.

Site No. 2: It was located at an altitude of 360 m and was a plantation of *Tectona grandis,* planted by State Forest Department some 15 years back with a few other species of trees. This site was surrounded by a cluster of huts constructed by gujjars (a muslim nomadic community) and was heavily grazed by their livestock. The ground vegetation was very sparse and dominated by forbs and weeds. The temperature at this site ranged between 12 ± 2 to 43 ± 3 C and relative humidity ranged between 19 to 89%.

Site No. 3: It was again a mixed forest like site no. 1 but at a little lower altitude (380m). It was inhabited by three gujjar families whose live stock lightly grazed the area. Temperature at this site ranged between 11 ± 2 to 38 ± 2 C while humidity ranged between 24 to 82%.

Site No. 4: This was a natural forest of *S. robusta*, with no encroachment by gujjars and their cattle. However, it appeared that some selective logging had been carried out in this site approximately 20 years back. The ground vegetation was represented mainly by *Cynodon dactylon, Veronia conizodes, Lygodium circinatum, Leucas mollissima, Ampelopteris prolifera* and *Achyranthus aspera.* The site was in the **Jamankhata Forest Block of the Sanctuary.** It was approximately 2.5 km away from the Hardwar-Dehradun railway line. The temperature and humidity ranged between 14 ± 2 to 36 ± 2C and 31 to 85% respectively.

STUDY OF SOME ABIOTIC PARAMETERS

Abiotic factors like temperature, humidity, soil pH, water absorbing capacity of the soil and organic matter in the soil have a great impact on the vegetation as well as on the fauna, particularly the entomofauna of an area. Keeping this fact in mind the atmospheric temperature and humidity of the area were recorded on each sampling date with the help of a thermohygrometer. The pH, organic matter and water absorbing capacity of the soil were determined on monthly basis and for this purpose soil samples from all the sites were collected and brought to the laboratory and each parameter mentioned above was determined as per the prescribed standard methods given by Michael (1984).

STUDY OF BIOTIC PARAMETERS

Analysis of Vegetation: A detailed survey of each of the study sites was carried out during different seasons in order to determine the vegetational composition. For the species of the plants which could not be identified in the field, herbariums were prepared and were got identified with the help of the Scientists from Botanical Survey of India, Dehradun, G. B. Pant Himalayan Research Institute, Kosi, Katarmal, Almora. Help of the forest department officials of Motichur Forest Range was also obtained for this purpose.

Collection of Entomofauna: The insects were collected by sweep sampling methods. Net sweeps were carried out in all the study sites. The nets used in the systematic sweeping were made of thick cotton cloths with a diameter of 30 cm. At the mouth and a bag length of 60 cm. Sampling was done as per Gadagkar et. al., 1990. For carrying out net sweeps, each site was divided in 100 quadrates each measuring in to 10 x 10 m. Six such quadrates were chosen at random and the entire area was covered during each sampling date. Sampling was done at an interval of 15 days between 8.00—13.00 hours. Collected insects were transferred in to bottles containing ethyl acetate soaked cotton. These bottles were brought to the laboratory and the insects were separated according to their systemic position, these were stretched, pinned and oven dried at 60°C for 72 hours in order to preserve them.

Insect Biomass: Biomass is defined as the live organic matter per unit area at a given point in time and is generally expressed in terms of oven dry weight per unit area (Odum, 1971). In the present study every insect is weighed in a single pan electric balance with an accuracy of 0.01 mg. Each dried and stretched insect was weighed along with its entomological pin with the help of balance and the average weight of the specific entomological pin used is subtracted from the insect weight to get the true value of biomass of an insects.

Trophic Structure: Once the insects were separated into different orders and got identified, these were categorised in to three groups *viz.*, Herbivorus, saprophagus and predators on the basis of their food habits.

Assessment of damage to the vegetation by entomofauna: To assess the damage caused by insects, a detailed survey of each of the study site and adjacent forest was carried out and a visual estimation of the damage being inflicted by the insects/pests was determined. The insects and different stages of their life cycles, causing the damage were collected and brought to the laboratory and culture was maintained to get the adult stages.

Application of plant extracts to see their effect on some of the pests: Neem leaves were selected to prepare a non-synthetic but active pesticide. To prepare the Neem extract, fresh new leaves were collected from trees growing on the Gurukul Kangri University Campus. The leaves were oven-dried at 60° C until they attained a constant weight. The dried leaves were ground into a powder using a mortar and pestle. Extracts of three different concentrations were prepared. Initially 100 mg of powder was added to 1 litre of distilled water at 22 ± 2°C for 24 h and strained through a piece of cotton cloth. This preparation was termed a 0.0001% extract (0.1 kg of powder added to 1,000 ml of water). To prepare 0.00006 and 0.00004% extracts respectively, 60 and 40 mg of powder were dissolved in the distilled water.

Fourth instar nymphs of the testgrasshopper, *O. velox*, were collected from the Rajaji National Park. Their principle food plant in this area, *Cynodon dactylon* L., was collected from the same area. Four replicates of each extract and an untreated control were used to assess the antifeedent effects in the laboratory at 29 ± 2°C, 77% RH, and 10:14 (L:D).

Record of Anthropogenic activities in the area : To understand the level and sources of disturbances caused by the different anthropogenic activities in the area, a survey chart containing different heads and questions was prepared. Survey of the entire Motichur Forest Range was also carried out to record the different factors and activities causing a disturbance in the forest ecosystem. Discussions with forest officials, Gujjars and with the people living in the peripheral areas of the sanctuary were also conducted on several occasions.

RESULTS

Results on the various abiotic and biotic parameters of this study have been given as under:

I. Abiotic Factors

1. Temperature and Humidity: During this period temperature varied from 14°C (1/2/99) to 40°C (1/6/97) in site no.1. In site no. 2 the minimum temperature was recorded on 2/1/98 (14°C) while the maximum was recorded on 1/6/97 (40°C). In site no. 3 minimum temperature was on 2/2/99 (11°C) and maximum was on 16/6/97 (35°C). In sites no. 4 the minimum and maximum temperature recorded were 12°C (2/2/99) and 36°C (2/6/97) respectively. Humidity varied from 80% (2/11/97) to 23% (1/5/99) in site no.1, from 70% (1/9/97) to 24% (1/5/99) in site no.2, from 82% (16/8/97) to 33% (16/4/98) in site no.3 and from 85% (2/9/97) to 27% (2/4/99) in site no. 4.

2. **pH, Water Absorbing capacity and Organic Matter in the Soil :** The minimum and maximum values on pH, water absorbing capacity and organic matter in soil during June 1997 to May 1999. The pH varied from 6.4 to 6.7, from 6.2 to 6.8, from 6.3 to 6.8 and from 6.4 to 6.8 in site no. 1,2,3 and 4 respectively. Similarly the water absorbing capacity which depends upon the fact that how much water is absorbed or retained by the given amount of soil, ranged from 31% to 39%, from 32% to 38%, from 32% to 37% and from 34% to 39% in site no. 1,2,3 and 4 respectively. Organic matter in soil varied from 1.96 –3.81%; from 2.01 – 3.18%; from 2.48 – 4.13% and from 2.70-4.80% in site no. 1,2,3 & 4 respectively.

II. Biotic Factor

1. **Floristic Composition:** A total of 97 species of plants (trees-16, shrubs-23 and herbs-58) were identified. Out of 97 specie, 75 species were present in the site no. 1. (Motichur forest block), 27 sepcies in site no. 2 (Koelpura forest block), 76 species in site no. 3 (Danda forest block) and 46 species in site no. 4 (Jamankhata forest block). All the species of plants were recorded during the rainy season (97) and far fewer were present during the winter (74) and summer season (69).

2. **Species Composition of Entomofauna:** A total of 150 species belonging to 47 families and 10 insect orders were collected during our study period. On the basis of number of individuals collected Lepidoptera was the most dominant order followed by Orthoptera and Coleoptera. The other orders reported from the study area include Hemiptera, Odonata, Hymenoptera, Diptera, Dictyoptera and Neuroptera. On the basis of number of species identified, order Lepidoptera is the most dominant order with 43 species followed by Hymenoptera, Odonata, Hemiptera and Coleoptera with 31,17, 16 and 16 species each, respectively. Seasonal variation in the species composition of different site is presented some of the important species collected from Motichur Sanctuary of Rajaji National Park.

Order Lepidoptera, was the most dominant insect order in terms of the number and species recorded and identified from the different study sites. This order was represented by 43 species belonging to 10 families. On the basis of number of individuals collected Pieridae was the most dominant family represented by 712 individuals of 9 species and *Terias hecabe hecabe* (Linn.) constituted 42.98% and *Catopsilia pomana,* 31.18% of the total number of individuals of this family. Family Satyridae was represented by 3 species and *Melanitis leda ismene* (Carmer) constituted 61.05% of the total number of individuals of this family. Family Nymphalidae was represented by 14 species and *Neptis yerburyi* But. and *Precis atlites* constituted 34.12% & 21.96%of the total number of individuals of this family respectively. Family Danaidae was represented by 5 species and *Euploea core core* (But.) constituted 47.74% of the total no. of individuals of this family.

Order Odonata was represented by 17 species. *Crocothemis servilia servilia* (Drury) was the most dominant odonate followed by ***Orthetrum chryostigma luzonicum*** (Brauer), *Trithemis festiva* Ramb. And *Orthetrum s. stigma* (Drury).

Order Coleoptera was represented by 16 species belonging to 7 families. Family Coccinellidae was the most dominant family with 268 individuals. *Rodolia guerinii* Crotch was the most abundant species constituting 32.08% of the total no. of individuals of this family. 202 individuals of family Scaraba-eidae belonging to 7 species were collected. Family Chrysome-lidae constituted 31.86% of the total coleopteran individuals collected during 1997-99 though it was represented by only one species, *Hoplasoma unicolar*b Tellig. constituting 81.60% of the total individuals of this family.

Order Heteroptera was represented by 16 species belonging to 5 families. Pyrrhocoridae, which was represented by 3 species, was the dominant family and *Physopelta schlanbuschi* was the dominant species of this family, constituting 77.78% of the total of this family. 5 species of family Coreidae were collected during the study period. *Leptocorisa* sp. Was the dominant species of this family, constituting 77.78% of the total of this family.

Order Orthroptera was represented by 14 species belonging to 3 families. Acrididae was the most dominant family, represented by 11 species. *Oxya velox* Fabr. was the most dominant species, followed by *Catantops humilis humilis* Serv., *Atractomorpha* sp., *Euprepocnemis alacris ceraria* sp. Family Tettigonidae was represented by 2 species and *Elimea* Species was the dominant species, while family Gryllidae was represented by *Gryllus* Species.

Order Hymenoptera was represented by 31 species belonging to 10 families. Family Vespidae was the most dominant family with 7 species. *Ropalidia ferruginia* (Fabr) and *Vespa a. affinis* were the dominant species. Family Scoliidae, with three species *Campsomeris phalerata* Sauss., *Campsomeris annulata* Fabr. and *Elis thoracica* was the second most dominant family.

Family Sphigidae was represented by 6 species and was dominated by *Ammophila atripes* Smith and *Sphex lobatus* Fabr.

Order Homoptera was represented by 4 species belonging to 3 families. On the basis of number of identified species and individuals family Cicadidae was the dominant family, which is represented by 2 species followed by Cicadellidae (1species) and Cercopidae (1species). *Scieroptera splendidula* Fabr. of family Cicadidae constituted 19.56% of the total number of individuals, collected of order Homoptera during 1997-99.

Order Diptera was represented by 3 species belonging to 2 families. Two species belonged to family Asilidae while one species belonged to family Tachinidae. On the basis of number of individuals family tachinidae was the dominant family though it was represented by only one species, *Winthemia* sp. Family Asilidae was dominated by *Machimus indianus* Ric. which constituted 62.50% of the total individuals of this family.

Order Dictyoptera was represented by 3 species

belonging to 2 families. Two species belonged to family Mantidae while to family Blattoidae. Family Blattoidae was the dominant family, as it constituted 87.60% of this order.

Order Neuroptera was represented by 3 species belonging to family Hemerobiidae. *Ogcogaster* sp. was the dominant species and constituted 53.34% of this family's total followed by *O. Tesselatus* Wet. and *Palpares pardus*.

3. Population Dynamics of Entomofauna: Data on total number of individuals and density per hectare on each sampling date from the study sites for a period of two years. Site wise variation in the density Vis-a-Vis variation in the temperature and humidity.

In Motichur forest block (Site no. 1), the density varied from 4.33 to 42.00 individuals/ha. In Koelpura forest block (Site no. 2), density ranged between 2.66 to 24.66 individuals/ha. In Danda forest block (Site no. 3), the minimum and maximum densities recorded were 3.33 individuals/ha and 27.00 individuals/ha while in Jamankhata forest block (Site no. 4), the density has ranged between 1.33 to 17.66 individuals/ha during 1997-98.

During 1998-99, the density ranged from 2.00-53.00 individuals/ha; 1.00-21.66 individuals/ha; 1.66-34.00 individuals/ha and 1.00-22.66 individuals/ha in site no. 1,2,3 & 4, respectively.

Order Lepidoptera was the most dominant order. The minimum and maximum densities (individuals/hectare) of lepidoptera, during 1997-98, ranged from 0.33 (15/1/98) to 9.00 (15/5/98); from 0.33 (15/6/98) to 9.00 (15/12/97); from 0.33 (2/7/97) to 15.00 (2/11/97) and from 0.33 (16/6/97) to 12.00 (16/6/97) in site no. 1,2,3 & 4, respectively.

During 1998-99 the minimum and maximum densities of lepidoptera ranged from 0.66 (1/12/99) to 43.33 (1/5/99); from 0.33 (1/12/98) to 9.33 (15/6/98); from 0.66 (12/2/99) to 14.00 (2/5/99) and from 1.00 (15/3/99) to 8.00 (2/8/99) in site no. 1,2,3 & 4, respectively. The minimum and maximum density of order Orthoptera during 1997-98, ranged from 1.33 (1/3/98) to 16.33 (15/10/97); from 0.33 (15/2/98) to 10.33 (15/10/97); from 0.66 (15/2/98) to 9.00 (2/9/97) and from 0.33 (16/

12/97) to 5.33 (16/5/98) in site no. 1,2,3 & 4, respectively.

During 1998-99 density of this order ranged from 0.66 (1/2/99) to 15.66 (15/5/99); from 0.33 (1/12/98) to 9.66 (1/9/98); from 0.33 (16/12/98) to 13.00 (2/9/98) and from 0.66 (16/3/99) to 6.66 (2/9/98) in site no. 1,2,3 & 4, respectively.

The minimum and maximum densities of Coleoptera during 1997-98, ranged from 0.33 (1/5/98) to 28.33 (1/11/97); from 0.33 (15/4/98) to 2.33 (1/5/98); from 0.33 (16/4/98) to 7.66 (16/8/98) and from 0.33 (16/12/97) to 9.33 (16/9/98) in site no. 1,2,3 & 4, respectively.

During 1998-99 the minimum and maximum density ranged from 0.33 (15/5/99) to 7.66 (15/6/98); from 0.33 (15/5/99) to 11.00 (1/7/98); from 0.33 (15/5/99) to 7.00 (2/6/98) and from 0.33 (2/11/98) to 8.66 (2/7/98) in site no. 1,2,3 & 4, respectively.

The minimum and maximum density of order Odonata during 1997-98, ranged from 0.33 (1/7/97) to 5.66 (15/3/98); from 0.33 (15/5/98) to 2.00 (1/11/97); from 0.33 (1/7/97) to 5.66 (2/12/97) and from 0.33 (2/8/97) to 2.00 (2/7/97) in site no. 1,2,3 & 4 respectively. While during 1998-99, it ranged from 0.33 (15/7/98) to 5.66 (15/3/99); from 0.33 (1/6/98) to 3.00 (1/8/98); from 0.33 (16/5/99) to 3.00 (2/12/98) and from 0.33 (16/5/99) to 3.66 (2/8/98) in site no. 1,2,3 & 4, respectively.

Density of Order Heteroptera ranged from 0.33 (15/10/97) to 20.33 (1/5/98); from 0.33 (15/8/97) to 1.66 (1/9/97); from 0.33 (2/11/97) to 8.33 (2/5/98) and from 0.33 (2/11/97) to 5.66 (2/6/97) in site no. 1,2,3 & 4 respectively during 1997-98 and from 0.33 (15/9/98) to 14.66 (15/3/99); from 0.33 (1/10/98) to 1.00 (15/7/98); from 0.33 (2/12/99) to 15.00 (2/5/99) and from 0.33 (16/12/98) t 2.66 (16/9/98) inosite no. 1,2,3 & 4, respectively during 1998-99.

Order Hymenoptera's minimum and maximum densities during 1997-98, ranged from 0.33 (15/6/97) to 3.33 (15/12/97); from 0.33 (1/9/97) to 2.66 (15/11/97); from 0.33 (2/6/97) to 2.33 (2/12/97) and from 0.33 (1/5/98) to 1.33 (15/6/97) in site no. 1,2,3 & 4 respectively. And during 1998-99 it ranged from 0.33 (15/2/99) to 1.00 (1/5/99); from 0.33 (15/6/98) to 2.00 (15/9/98); from 0.33 (2/9/98) to 1.66 (2/6/98) and

0.33 in site no. 1,2,3 & 4, respectively.

Order Homoptera's minimum and maximum densities during 1997-98, ranged from 0.33 (15/7/97) to 1.33 (1/8/97); from 0.33 (1/10/97) to 0.66 (15/7/97); from 0.66 (2/9/97) to 2.00 (2/7/97) and from 0.33 (16/8/97) to 2.00 (2/8/97) in site no. 1,2,3 & 4, respectively.

While during 1998-99 it ranged from 0.33 (15/6/98) to 0.66 (15/7/98); 1.33 (1/7/98); from 0.66 (16/7/98) to 6.33 (2/8/98) and from 0.33 (16/6/98) to 3.66 (2/7/98) in site no. 1,2,3 & 4, respectively.

Order Diptera's minimum and maximum densities durıng 1997-98 ranged from 0.33 (15/5/98) to 8.00 (15/10/97); from 0.33 (1/5/98) to 5.33 (1/9/97); from 0.33 (16/8/97) to 4.00 (16/11/97) and from 0.33 (16/12/97) to 4.00 (2/4/98) in site no. 1,2,3 & 4 respectively, during 1998-99 it was from 0.33 (15/2/99) to 3.33 (1/5/99); from 0.33 (15/2/99) to 1.33 (1/4/99); from 0.33 (16/12/98) to 5.00 (2/4/99) and from 0.33 (16/12/98) to 1.00 (16/3/99) in site no. 1,2,3 & 4, respectively.

The minimum and maximum densities of order Neuroptera during 1997-98, ranged from 1.33 (15/8/97) to 3.33 (1/8/97); from 0.33 (15/8/98) to 1.66 (15/9/97); from 0.33 (16/10/97) to 5.00 (16/8/97) and from 0.33 (16/10/97) to 1.00 (2/8/97) in site no. 1,2,3 & 4 respectively and during 1998-99 densities ranged from 0.33 (1/7/98) to 0.66 (1/8/98); from 0.33 (15/9/98) to 0.66 (15/7/98); from 0.66 (2/7/98) to 3.00 (16/9/98) and 0.33 (16/6/98 & 16/9/98) in site no. 1,2,3 & 4, respectively.

Order Dictyoptera's minimum and maximum density, during 1997-98, ranged from 0.33 (15/12/97) to 0.66 (1/7/97); from 0.33 (15/3/98) to 0.66 (15/7/97); from 0.33 (16/10/97) to 1.00 (2/6/97) and from 0.33 (2/4/98) to 1.00 (2/6/97) in site no. 1,2,3 & 4 respectively. While during 1998-99 minimum and maximum density was 0.33 (15/4/99) in site no. 1; from 0.33 (16/3/99) to 1.00 (16/6/98) in site no. 3 and 0.33 in site no. 4.

4. Biomass of insects: The variation in the biomass (mg/hect.) and density (/hect.) during 1997-98 and 1998-99. During 1997-98 biomass of insects varied from 3165.1 mg/hect. (01/11/97) to 233.8 (01/03/98) mg/hect. in site no.1, from

2936.3 mg/hect. (15/10/97) to 57.3 mg/hect. (15/02/98) in site no. 2, from 1729.9 mg/hect. (02/10/97) to 144.3 mg/hect. (02/02/98) in site no.3 while from 1259.1 mg/hect. (16/05/98) to 40.2 mg/hect. (03/01/98) in site no.4.

During 1998-99 biomass of insects varied from 3960.0 mg/hect. (01/05/99) to 111.0 mg/hect. (02/01/99) in site no.1, from 2388.4 mg/hect. (15/06/98) to 13.0 mg/hect. (01/02/99) in site no.2, from 2619.8 mg/hect. (02/08/98) to 40.1 mg/hect. (02/02/99) in site no.3 while from 1521.1 mg/hect. (02/09/98) to 31.9 mg/hect. (02/03/99) in site no.4.

5. Species Diversity: The richness and variety of a natural community can be described as "Diversity" whereas the ratio between number of species and importance value of individuals is called "Species Diversity" indices of the total number of species (Odum, 1971). In a community, a relatively small percentage of the organisms are usually abundant and they have large importance value, whereas a large percentage are rare and have small importance value. The total species diversity of Motichur forest range was 5.560 during 1997-98 while it was 5.472 during 1998-99.

6.Trophic Structure: The food of forest insects is the most important characteristic feature. From the functional point of view, a population can be analysed into many terms, one of which is the food chain. Insects feed on a variety of food plants. Hence the present insect population has been categorised into three groups *i.e.*, herbivores, predators and saprophages.

It is a very well known fact that herbivores dominate all the food chains and food webs, in terms of number of individuals and species collected of any ecosystem. It is clear from table 10 that during 1997-99, herbivores (77.52%) constituted of the total individuals collected followed by predators (18.30) and saprophages (4.18).

During 1997-99, the herbivore species constituted 53.41% of the total species collected followed by predators (43.08) and saprophages (3.85).

7. **Insect Pests and Damage:** Though, the damage may be a part of the natural cycles of food and feeding by the

herbivorous insects, however, in some cases where the population of the pests dominates, it may reflect to the health of the forest.

The larvae of *Pieris canida* Sparr. and *Hyblea puera* Cramer were collected from the site no. 2 (Koelpura forest block) on the leaves of *Tectona grandis*. The culture of these larvae was maintained in the laboratory to know the pest insect. The second and third instar larvae feed on the leaves of teak very vigorously leaving behind the venation net work of leaves while the later instars feed the entire leaves.

Some other larval stages of different lepidopteran pests were also collected from teak and *Mallotus philippinensis* during the rainy season but the culture of these was not a successful venture. These larval stages were got identified as *Sphinx lingustri* Linn. (Lepidoptera: Phingidae); *Biston betularia* Linn. (Lepidoptera: Geometridae); *Hyblea puera* Cramer and one larvae of Arctiidae family from Entomological Division of Forest Research Institute, Dehradun.

During the rainy season, the infestation of *Hyblea puera* was widely noticed, destroying the leaves of teak and hindering its growth.

Oxya velox Fabr. (Orthoptera: Acrididae) was found feeding extensively on the leaves of the *Sohrea robusta. Catantops h. humilis* Serv., *C. innotabile* Wlk. and *Euprepocnemis alacris* Swrv. (Acrididae) were some other important pests of teak while *Chrotogonus* sp. was of *Dalbergia sissoo. Gryllus* sp. (Orthoptera : Gryllidae) is an omnivorous species which feeds on seeds and small seedlings.

Cantao ocellatus (Thunberg) (Hemiptera : Scutelleridae) and *Physopelta schlanbuschi* Fabr. (Hemiptera : Pyrrhocoridae), were observed feeding extensively on the fruits and seeds of *Mallotus philippinesis* and thus inflicting damage. During the months of May and June, in scorching sun and just before the onset of monsoon, their density in site no. 1 (Motichur forest block) was amazing on the small trees of *Mallotus* during both the study years *i.e.*, 1997-98 & 1998-99. The first, second and third instar of *Physopelta schlanbuschi* and *P. gutta* live under the litter in the daytime to avoid the excessive heat while fourth to adult instars can be seen easily on the twigs and leaves in the mating posture.

Stromatium barbatum (Coleoptera : Cerambycidae) is a well known shoot borer of sal. The number of its individuals were few and not in alarming density in the study area.

Some pupal moult cover of sal borer *Hoplocerambyx sponicornis*, were found on sal tree trunks, but no alive specimen could be traced. Though in some far and remote areas, this pest was reported by local gujjars, but could not be traced in Motichur forest area.

Mylarbis pustulata Thun., *Oxycetonia albopunctata* Thun. and *Cetoniinae* sp. (Coleoptera : Scarabaeidae) are the general pests of flowers and leaves of many plants of different families.

Haphsa nichomache Wlk. (Homoptera : Cicadidae) is a sap sucker of chilbil. It can be heard easily in the forest during the day time.

ANTHROPOGENIC ACTIVITIES

A survey of the various anthropogenic activities within the Motichur forest range was carried out. There were recorded two types of anthropogenic activities in the forest area. One was of the people, living in peripheral villages of Motichur forest range while another was of forest Gujjars, Muslim nomadic grazier, settled inside the forest. To understand the pressure of these villages and gujjars on the forest and forest resources, a detailed study of their family structure, distribution of families, literacy and their livestock was carried out. Specially the kind of activities carried out by the gujjar families were surveyed.

FOREST GUJJARS

Family Structure: During this period a total of 57 families of gujjars living in the different blocks of the Motichur Range were identified. On an average a gujjar family has 8 members, which includes 3-4 adults and 4-5 children (below the age of 14 years). Mostly these families have their huts close to a perennial source of water. The total population of these families was found 423 with 238 children and 185 adults. Most of the family members are still illiterate with a very little knowledge of reading and writing or both.

Live Stock: Maintaining a good number of cattle population is being practised by each of the gujjar families. Each family has 3-6 buffaloes, 2-3 buffalo calves, 2-3 cows, 1-2 cow calves, 3-4 goats and some families do posses 1-2 bulls. The animals appear under nourished, though the gujjars are highly dependent on their cattle as far as their economy is concerned. The normal range of milk yield in the area was 3-4 litres per cattle.

Use of Forest Resources: Being at the heart of each forest block, the resources (fuels, fodder, and timber) are easily available to the gujjars. However, it seems that they are also maintaining the environment of their areas in their own ways. As the area close to their deras appear to be more green with healthy vegetation. The fodder is mainly collected by lopping of the trees, and the species which are mainly lopped for this purpose include; Kachnar (*Piliostigma malabericum*), Bakail (*Anegeisus latifolia*), bahera (*Terminalia belerica*).

There is no fixed time as far as looping is concerned, whenever the need is felt the activity is repeated. The wood is also utilised in a routine manner for cooking and heating purposes. Plenty of dead wood was also seen in the area during our visits for insect collection purposes. Though dead wood is collected for fuel but lopping of the trees is also very common practice to collect the fuel wood. Some lopping of good quality of trees is also carried out (on very few occasions) to sell them to the people living in the peripheral areas. The grazing by cattle is very extensive. The cattle are left free in the area and they cover approximate 3-4kms each day, thus removing the grasses of the area completely.

PEOPLE OF PERIPHERAL AREA

Villages from two sides surround Motichur forest range and the villages on its periphery are mainly Raywala,

Satyanarayan, Motichur and Haripur Kalan. The main population of these villages is composed of the migrated people of Tehri and its adjacent area, which were displaced duo to the construction of Tehri dam. The land, which is allotted to them in this area, belonged to the Forest Department and it would have been a part of Rajaji National Park. The economic condition of these people is not very good and most of these families are completely dependent on the forest resources for fuel, fodder and timber.

The lopping of green trees for fodder, fuel and timber is a very common practice for these families though a good amount of dead wood is available easily in the forest area. The effects of collection of different forest resources by these people from the park area adjacent to these villages, can clearly be noticed. The people lope trees many times in a year and thus not permitting them to flower. As a result, the canopy cover and density of trees is decreasing in such areas very sharply.

Females of these families were seen collecting fodder and fuel wood throughout the year, except during rainy season. They cover far and flung areas in the summer, when there is acute shortage of fodder. Excessive lopping of some popular fodder tree species have threatened their survival, as flowering is not possible due to regular lopping.

The cattle of these villages, which comprise mainly of cows and buffaloes, are set free in the morning to graze in the forest and are collected in the evening. These cattle approximately cover an area of 3-4 km daily and graze or destroy the ground vegetation and young seedlings. In a natural system, though the growth and recycling of different communities and nutrients takes place naturally but if the communities are not allowed to grow and propagate due to excessive biotic pressures the natural phenomena also gets disturbed leading to crunch of resources in due course of time.

8

The Convention on Biological Diversity

During the historic United Nations Conference on Environment and Development (UNCED) also known as the Earth Summit held in Rio-de-Janerio in Brazil from 3rd to 14th June, 1992 following important documents were adopted:

(i) Rio Declaration
(ii) Agenda 21
(iii) Non-legally binding Principles on Forests
(iv) Frame work Convention on Climate Change
(v) Convention on Biological Diversity
(vi) Agreement to negotiate a convention on Desertification.

While the two conventions are legally binding international instruments for the parties, the first three documents are non-binding. The convention on Biological Diversity, which was signed by 171 countries including India during Rio and thereafter, has entered into force with effect from 29th December, 1993. India has ratified the convention on 18th February, 1994 and thus it has come into force for India from 19th May 1994 *i.e.,* after 90 days of the ratification.

THE CONVENTION ON BIOLOGICAL DIVERSITY

Conscious of the intrinsic value of biological diversity

and of the Ecological, Genetic, Social, Economic, Scientific, Educational, Cultural, Recreational and Aesthetic values of biological diversity and its components, Conscious also of the importance of biological diversity for evolution and for maintaining life-sustaining systems of the biosphere, affirming that the conservation of biological diversity is a common concern of humankind, reaffirming that States has sovereign rights over their own biological resources, reaffirming also that States are responsible for conserving there Biological diversity and for using their biological resources in a sustainable manncr, concerned that biological diversity is being significantly reduced by certain human activities, aware of the general lack of information and knowledge regarding Biological diversity and of the urgent need to develop scientific, technical and institutional capacities to provide the basic understanding upon which to plan and implement appropriate measures, noting that it is vital to anticipate, prevent and attack the causes of significant reduction or loss of biological diversity at source, noting also that where there is a threat of significant reduction or loss of biological diversity, lack of full scientific certainty should not be used as a reason for postponing measures to avoid or minimize such a threat, noting further that the fundamental requirement for the conservation of biological diversity is the in-situ conservation of ecosystems and natural habitats and the maintenance and recovery of viable populations of species in their natural surroundings, noting further that ex-situ measures, preferably in the country of origin, also have an important role to play, recognizing the close and traditional dependence of many indigenous and local communities embodying traditional lifestyles on biological resources, and the desirability of sharing equitably benefits arising from the use of traditional knowledge, innovations and practices relevant to the conservation of biological diversity and the sustainable use of its components, recognizing also the vital role that women play in the conservation and Sustainable use of biological diversity and affirming the need for the full participation of women at all levels of policy-making and implementation for biological diversity conservation.

Stressing the importance of, and the need to promote, international, regional and global cooperation among States and inter-governmental organizations and the non-governmental sector for the conservation of biological diversity and the sustainable use of its components.

Acknowledging that the provision of new and additional financial resources and appropriate access to relevant technologies can be expected to make a substantial difference in the world's ability to address the loss of biological diversity.

Acknowledging further that special provision is required to meet the needs of developing countries, including the provision of new and additional financial resources and appropriate access to relevant technologies.

Noting in this regard the special conditions of the least developed countries and Small Island States.

Acknowledging that substantial investments are required to conserve biological diversity and that there is the expectation of a broad range of environmental, economic and social benefits from those investments.

Recognizing that economic and social development and poverty eradication are the first and overriding priorities of developing countries.

Aware that conservation and sustainable use of biological diversity is of critical importance for meeting the food, health and other need of the growing world population, for which purpose access to and sharing of both genetic resources and technologies are essential.

Noting that, ultimately, the conservation and sustainable use of biological diversity will strengthen friendly relations among States and contribute to peace for humankind,

Desiring to enhance and complement existing international arrangements for the conservation of biological diversity and sustainable use of its components, and

Determined to conserve and sustainably use biological

diversity for the benefit of present and future generations.

1. Objectives

The objectives of this Convention, to be pursued in accordance with its relevant provisions, are the conservation of biological diversity, the sustainable use of its components and the fair and equitable sharing of the benefits arising out of the utilization of genetic resources, including by appropriate access to genetic resources and by appropriate transfer of relevant technologies, taking into account all rights over those resources to technologies, and by appropriate funding.

2. Use *of* Terms

For the purposes of this Convention: "Biological diversity" means the variability among living organisms from all sources including, *inter alia*, terrestrial, marine and other aquatic, ecosystems and the ecological complexes "Biotechnology" means any technological application that uses biological systems, living organisms, or derivatives thereof, to make or modify products or processes for specific use.

"Country of origin of genetic resources" means the country, which possesses those genetic resources in *in-situ* conditions.

"Country providing genetic resources" means the country supplying genetic resource, collected from *in-situ* sources, including populations of both wild and domesticated species, or taken from *ex-situ* sources, which mayor may not have originated in that country.

"Domesticated or *cultivated species"* means species in which the evolutionary process has been influenced by humans to meet their needs.

"Ecosystem" means a dynamic complex of plant, animal and microorganism communities and their non-living environment interacting as a functional unit.

Ex-situ conservation means the conservation of components of biological diversity outside their natural habitats.

"Genetic material" means any material of plant, animal, microbial or other origin containing functional units of heredity.

"Genetic resources" means genetic material of actual or potential value.

"Habitat" means the place or type of site where an organism or population naturally occurs.

"In-situ" conditions means conditions where genetic resources exist within ecosystems and natural habitats, and in the case of domesticated or cultivated species in the surroundings where they have developed their distinctive properties.

"Protected area" means a geographically defined area which is designated or regulated and managed to achieve specific conservation objectives.

"Regional economic integration organization" means an organization constituted by sovereign States of a given region, to which its member states have transferred competence in respect of matters governed by this Convention and which has been duly authorized, in accordance with its internal procedures, to sign, ratify, accept, approve or accede to it.

Sustainable use means the use of components of biological diversity in a way and at a rate that does not lead to the long-term decline of biological diversity, thereby maintaining its potential to meet the needs and aspirations of presents and future generations.

"Technology" includes biotechnology.

3. Principle

States have, in accordance with the Charter of the United Nations and the principles of international law, the sovereign right to exploit their own resources pursuant to their own environmental policies, and the responsibility to ensure that activities within their jurisdiction or control do not cause damage to the environment of other States or of areas beyond the limits of national jurisdiction.

4. Jurisdictional Scope

Subject to the rights of other States, and except as otherwise expressly provided in this Convention, the provisions of this Convention apply, in relation to each Contracting Party:

(*a*) In the case of components of biological diversity, in areas within the limits of its national jurisdiction; and

(*b*) In the case of processes and activities, regardless of where their effects occur, carried out under its jurisdiction or control, within the area of its national jurisdiction or beyond the limits of national jurisdiction.

5. Co-operation

Each Contracting Party shall, as far as possible and as appropriate, cooperate with other Contracting Parties, directly or, where appropriate, through competent international organizations, in respect of areas beyond national jurisdiction and on other matters of mutual interest, for the conservation and sustainable use of biological diversity.

6. General Measures for Conservation and Sustainable Use

Each Contracting Party shall, in accordance with its particular conditions and capabilities:

(*a*) Develop national strategies, plans or programmes for the conservation and sustainable use of biological diversity or adapt for this purpose existing strategies, plans or programmes which shall reflect, *inter alia,* the measures set out in this Convention relevant to the Contracting Party concerned; and

(*b*) Integrate, as far as possible and as appropriate, the conservation and sustainable use of biological diversity into relevant sectoral or cross-sectoral plans, programmes and policies.

7. Identification and Monitoring

Each contracting Party shall, as far as possible and as appropriate, in particular for the purposes of Articles 8 to 10:

(*a*) Identify components of biological diversity important for its conservation and sustainable use having regard to the indicative list of categories set down in Annex I;

(*b*) Monitor, through sampling and other techniques, the components of biological diversity identified pursuant to subparagraph (a) above, paying particular attention to those requiring urgent conservation measures and those which offer the greatest potential for sustainable use;

(*c*) Identify processes and categories of activitics which have or are likely to have significant adverse impacts on the conservation and sustainable use of biological diversity, and monitor their effects through sampling and other techniques; and

(*d*) Maintain and organize, by any mechanism data, derived from identification and monitoring activities pursuant to subparagraphs (a), (b) and (c) above.

8. *In-situ conservation*

Each contracting party shall, as far as possible and as appropriate.

(*a*) Establish a system of protected areas or areas where special measures need to be taken to conserve biological diversity;

(*b*) Develop, where necessary, guidelines for the selection establishment and management of protected areas or areas where special measure need to be taken to conserve biological diversity;

(*c*) Regular or manage biological resources important for the conservation of biological diversity whether within or outside protected areas with a view to ensuring their conservation and a sustainable use;

(d) Promote the protection of ecosystems natural habitats and the maintenance of viable populations species in natural surroundings;

(e) Promote environmentally sound and sustainable development in areas adjacent to protected areas with a view to furthering protection of these areas;

(f) Rehabilitate and restore degraded ecosystems and promote the recovery of threatened species inter alia, through the development and implementation of plans or other management strategies;

(g) Establish or maintain means to regulate, manage or control the risks associated with the use and release of living modified organisms, resulting from biotechnology which are likely to have adverse environmental impacts that could affect the conservation and sustainable use of biological diversity taking also into account the risks to human health;

(h) Prevent the introduction of control or eradicate those alien species which threaten ecosystems habitats or species;

(i) Endeavour to provide the conditions needed for compatibility between present uses and the conservation of biological diversity and the sustainable use of its components;

(j) Subject to its national legislation, respect, preserve and maintain knowledge, innovations and practices of indigenous and local communities embodying traditional lifestyles relevant for the conservation and sustainable use of biological diversity and promote their wider application with the approval and involvement of the holders of such knowledge, innovations and practices and encourage the equitable sharing of the benefits arising from the utilization of such knowledge, innovations and practices;

(k) Develop or maintain necessary legislation and/or other regulatory provisions for the protection of threatened species and populations.

(l) Where a significant adverse effect on biological diversity has been determined pursuant to Article 7, regulate or manage the relevant processes and categories of activities; and

(m) Cooperate in providing financial and other support for *in-situ* conservation outlined in subparagraphs (a) to (1) above, particularly to developing countries.

9. Ex-situ Conservation

Each Contracting Party shall, as far as possible and as appropriate, and predominantly for the purpose of complementing *in-situ* measures:

(a) Adopt measures for the *ex-situ* conservation of components of biological diversity, preferably in the country of origin of such components;

(b) Establish and maintain facilities for *ex-situ* conservation of and research on plants, animals and micro-organisms, preferably in the country of origin of genetic resources;

(c) Adopt measures for the recovery and rehabilitation of threatened species and for their reintroduction into their natural habitats under appropriate conditions;

(d) Regulate and manage collection of biological resources from natural habitats for *ex-situ* conservation purposes so as not to threaten ecosystems and *in-situ* populations of species, except where special temporary *ex-situ* measures are required under subparagraph (C) above; and

(e) Co-operate in providing financial and other support for *ex-situ* conservation outlined in subparagraphs (a) to (d) above and in the establishment and maintenance of *ex-situ* conservation facilities in developing countries.

10. Sustainable Use of Components of Biological Diversity

Each Contracting Party shall, as far as possible and as appropriate:

(a) Integrate consideration of the conservation and sustainable use of biological resources into national decision-making;

(b) Adopt measures relating to the use of biological resources to avoid or minimize adverse impacts on biological diversity;

(c) Protect and encourage customary use of biological resources in accordance with traditional cultural practices that are compatible with conservation or sustainable use requirements;

(d) Support local populations to develop and implement remedial action in degraded areas where biological diversity has been reduced; and

(e) Encourage co-operation between its governmental authorities and its private sector in developing methods for sustainable use of biological resources.

11. Incentive Measures

Each contracting Party shall, as far as possible and as appropriate, adopt economically and socially sound measures that act as incentives for the conservation and sustainable use of components of biological diversity.

12. Research and Training

The Contracting Parties, taking into account the special needs of developing countries, shall:

(a) Establish and maintain programmes for scientific and technical education and training in measures for the identification, conservation and sustainable use of biological diversity and its components and provide support for such education and training for the specific needs of developing countries;

(b) Promote and encourage research which contributes to the conservation and sustainable use of biological diversity, particularly in developing countries, *inter alia,* in accordance with decisions of the Conference of the Parties taken in consequence of recommendations of the Subsidiary Body on Scientific, Technical and Technological Advice; and

(c) In keeping with the provisions of Articles 16, la and 20, promote and cooperate in the use of scientific advances in biological diversity research in developing methods for conservation and sustainable use of biological resources.

13. Public Education and Awareness

The Contracting Parties shall:

(a) Promote and encourage understanding of the importance of, and the measures required for, the conservation of biological diversity, as well as its propagation through media, and the inclusion of these topics in educational programmes; and

(b) Cooperate, as appropriate, with other States and international organizations in developing educational and public awareness programmes, with respect to conservation and sustainable use of biological diversity.

14. Impact Assessment and Minimizing Adverse Impacts

1. Each Contracting Party, as far as possible and as appropriate, shall:

   (a) Introduce appropriate procedures requiring environmental impact assessment of its proposed projects that are likely to have significant adverse effects on biological diversity with a view to avoiding or minimizing such effects and, where appropriate, allow for public participation in such procedures;

   (b) Introduce appropriate arrangements to ensure that the environmental consequences of its programmes and policies that are likely to have significant adverse impacts on biological diversity are duly taken into account;

(c) Promote, on the basis of reciprocity, notification, exchange of information and consultation on activities under their jurisdiction or control which are likely to significantly affect adversely the biological diversity of other States or areas beyond the limits of national jurisdiction, by; encouraging the conclusion of bilateral, regional or multilateral, arrangements, as appropriate;

(d) In the case of imminent or grave danger or damage, originating under its jurisdiction or control, to biological diversity within the area under jurisdiction of other States or in areas beyond the limits of national jurisdiction, notify immediately the potentially affected States of such danger or damage, as well as initiate action to prevent or minimize such danger or damage; and

(e) Promote national arrangements for emergency responses to activities or events, whether caused naturally or otherwise, which present a grave and imminent danger to biological diversity and encourage international cooperation to supplement such national efforts and, where appropriate and agreed by the States or regional economic integration organizations concerned, to establish joint contingency plans.

2. The Conference of the Parties shall examine, on the basis of studies to be carried out, the issue of liability and redress, including restoration and compensation, for damage to biological diversity, except where such liability is a purely internal matter.

15. Access to Genetic Resources

1. Recognizing the sovereign rights of states over their natural resources, the authority to determine access to genetic resources rests with the national governments and *is* subject to national legislation.
2. Each Contracting Party shall endeavour to create

conditions to facilitate access to genetic resources for environmentally bound uses by other Contracting Parties and not to impose restrictions that run counter to the objectives of this convention.

3. For the purpose of this Convention, the genetic resources being provided, by a Contracting Party, as referred to in this Article and Articles 16 and 19, are only those that are provided by Contracting Parties that are countries of origin of such resources or by the Parties that have acquired the genetic resources in accordance with this Convention.
4. Access, where granted, shall be on mutually agreed terms and subject to the provisions of this Article.
5. Access to genetic resources shall be subject to prior informed consent of the Contracting Party providing such resources, unless otherwise determined by that Party.
6. Each Contracting Party shall endeavour to develop and carry out scientific research based on genetic resources provided by other Contracting Parties with the full participation of, and where possible in, such Contracting Parties.
7. Each contracting Party shall take legislative, administrative or policy measures, as appropriate, and in accordance with Articles 16 and 19 ánd, where necessary, through the financial mechanism established by Articles 20 and 21 with the aim of sharing in a fair and equitable way the results of research and development and the benefits arising from the commercial and other utilization of genetic resources with the Contracting Party providing such resources. Such sharing shall be upon mutually agreed terms.

16. Access to and Transfer of Technology

1. Each Contracting Party, recognizing that technology includes biotechnology, and that both access to and transfer of technology among Contracting Parties are

essential elements for the attainment of the objectives of this Convention, undertakes subject to the provisions of this Article to provide and/or facilitate access for and transfer to other Contracting Parties of technologies that are relevant to the conservation and sustainable use of biological diversity or make use of genetic resources and do not cause significant damage to the environment.

2. Access to and transfer of technology referred to in paragraph 1 above to developing countries shall be provided and/or facilitated under fair and most favourable terms, including on concessional and preferential terms where mutually agreed, and, where necessary, in accordance with the financial mechanism established by Articles 20 and 21. In the case of technology subject to patents and other intellectual property rights, such access and transfer shall be provided on terms which recognize and are consistent with the adequate and effective protection of intellectual property rights. The application of this paragraph shall be consistent with paragraphs 3, 4 and 5 below.
3. Each Contracting Party shall take legislative, administrative or policy measures, as appropriate, with the aim that Contracting Parties, in particular those that are developing countries, which provide genetic resources are provided access to and transfer of technology which makes use of those resources, on mutually agreed terms, including technology protected by patents and other intellectual property rights, where necessary, through the provisions of Articles 20 and 21 and in accordance with international law and consistent with paragraphs 4 and 5 below.
4. Each Contracting Party shall take legislative, administrative or policy measures, as appropriate, with the aim that the private sector facilitates access to, joint development and transfer of technology

referred to in paragraph 1 above for the benefit of both governmental institutions and the private sector of developing countries and in this regard shall abide by the obligations included in paragraphs 1,2 and 3 above.

5. The Contracting Parties, recognizing that patents and other intellectual property rights may have an influence on the implementation of this Convention, shall cooperate in this regard subject to national legislation and international law in order to ensure that such rights are supportive of and do not run counter to its objectives.

17. Exchange of Information

1. The Contracting Parties shall facilitate the exchange of information, from all publicly available sources, relevant to the conservation and sustainable use of biological diversity, taking into account the special needs of developing countries.
2. Such exchange of information shall include exchange of results of technical, scientific and socio-economic research, as well as information on training and surveying programmes, specialized knowledge, indigenous and traditional knowledge as such and in combination with the technologies referred to in Article 16, paragraph 1. It shall also, where feasible, include repatriation of information.

18. Technical and Scientific Cooperation

1. The Contracting Parties shall promote international technical and scientific cooperation in the field of conservation and sustainable use of biological diversity, where necessary, through the appropriate international and national institutions.
2. Each Contracting Party shall promote technical and scientific cooperation with other contracting Parties, in particular developing countries, in implementing this Convention, *inter alia,* through the development

and implementation of national policies. In promoting such cooperation, special attention should be given to the development and strengthening of national capabilities, by means of human resources development and institution building.

3. The Conference of the Parties, at its first meeting, shall determine how to establish a clearing-house mechanism to promote and facilitate technical and scientific cooperation.
4. The Contracting Parties shall, in accordance with national legislation and policies, encourage and develop methods of cooperation for the development and use of technologies, including indigenous and traditional technologies, in pursuance of the objectives of this Convention. For this purpose, the Contracting Parties shall also promote cooperation in the training of personnel and exchange of experts.
5. The Contracting Parties shall, subject to mutual agreement, promote the establishment of joint research programmes and joint ventures for the development of technologies relevant to the objectives of this Convention.

19. Handling of Biotechnology and Distribution of its Benefits

1. Each contracting party shall take legislative, administrative or policy measures, as appropriate, to provide for the effective participation in biotechnological research activities by those Contracting Parties, especially developing countries, which provide the genetic resources for such research, and where feasible in such Contracting Parties.
2. Each Contracting Party shall take all practicable measures to promote and advance priority access on a fair and equitable basis by Contracting Parties, especially developing countries, to the results and benefits arising from biotechnologies based upon

genetic resources provided by those Contracting Parties. Such access shall be on mutually agreed terms.

3. The Parties shall consider the need for and modalities of a protocol setting out appropriate procedures, including, in particular, advance informed agreement, in the field of the safe transfer, handling and use of any living modified organism resulting from biotechnology that may have adverse effect on the conservation and sustainable use of biological diversity.
4. Each Contracting Party shall, directly or by requiring any natural or legal person under its jurisdiction providing the organisms referred to in paragraph 3 above, provide any available information about the use and safety regulations required by that Contracting Party in handling such organisms, as well as any available information on the potential adverse impact of the specific organisms concerned to the Contracting Party into which those organisms are to be introduced.

20. Financial Resources

1. Each Contracting Party undertakes to provide, in accordance with its capabilities, financial support and incentive in respect of those national activities which are intended to achieve the objectives of this Convention, in accordance with its national plans, priorities and programmes.
2. The developed country Parties shall provide new and additional financial resources to enable developing country Parties to meet the agreed full incremental costs to them of implementing measures which fulfil the obligations of this Convention and to benefit from its provisions and which costs are agreed between a developing country Party and the institutional structure referred to in Article 21, in accordance with policy, strategy, programme priorities and eligibility

criteria and an indicative list of incremental costs established by the Conference of the Parties. Other parties, including countries undergoing the process of transition to a market economy, may voluntarily assume the obligations of the developed country Parties. For the purpose of this Article, the Conference of the Parties, shall at its first meeting establish a list of developed country Parties and other Parties, which voluntarily assume the obligations of the developed country Parties. The Conference of the Parties shall periodically review and if necessary amend the list. Contributions from other countries and sources on a voluntary basis would also be encouraged. The implementation of these commitments shall take into account the need for adequacy, predictability and timely flow of funds and the importance of burden-sharing among the contributing Parties included in the list.

3. The developed country Parties may also provide, and developing country Parties avail themselves of, financial resources related to the implementation of this Convention through bilateral, regional and other multilateral channels.
4. The extent to which developing country Parties will effectively implement their commitments under this Convention will depend on the effective implementation by developed country Parties of their commitments under this Convention related to financial resources and transfer of technology and will take fully into account the fact that economic and social development and eradication of poverty are the first and overriding priorities of the developing country Parties.
5. The Parties shall take full account of the specific needs and special situation of least developed countries in their actions with regard to funding and transfer of technology.
6. The Contracting Parties shall also take into

consideration the special conditions resulting from the dependence on, distribution and location of, biological diversity within developing country Parties, in particular small island States.

7. Consideration shall also be given to the special situation of developing countries, including those that are most environmentally vulnerable, such as those with arid and semi-arid zones, coastal and mountainous areas.

21. Financial Mechanism

1. There shall be a mechanism for the provision of financial resources to developing country Parties for purposes of this Convention on a grant or concessional basis the essential elements of which are described in this Article. The mechanism shall function under the authority and guidance of, and be accountable to, the Conference of the Parties for purposes of this Convention. The operations of the mechanism shall be carried out by such institutional structure as may be decided upon by the conference of the Parties at its first meeting. For purposes of this Convention, the Conference of the Parties shall determine the policy, strategy, programme priorities and eligibility criteria relating to the access to and utilization of such resources. The contributions shall be such as to take into account the need for predictability, adequacy and timely flow of funds referred to in Article 20 in accordan e with the amount of resources needed to be decided periodically by the Conference of the Parties and the importance of burden-sharing among the Contributing Parties included in the list referred to in Article 20, paragraph 2. Voluntary contributions may also be made by the developed country Parties and by other countries and sources. The mechanism shall operate within a democratic and transparent system of governance.

2. Pursuant to the objective of this convention, the Conference of the Parties shall at its first meeting determine the policy, strategy and programme priorities, as well as detailed criteria and guidelines for eligibility for access to and utilization of the financial resources including monitoring and evaluation on a regular basis of such utilization. The Conference of the Parties shall decide on the arrangements to give effect to paragraph 1 above after consultation with the institutional structure entrusted with the operation of the financial mechanism.
3. The Conference of the Parties shall review the effectiveness of the mechanism established under this Article, including the criteria and guidelines referred to in paragraph 2 above, not less than two years after the entry into force of this Convention and thereafter on a regular basis. Based on such review, it shall take appropriate action to improve the effectiveness of the mechanism if necessary.
4. The Contracting Parties shall consider strengthening existing financial institutions to provide financial resources for the conservation and sustainable use of biological diversity.

22. Relationship with Other International Conventions

1. The provisions of this Convention shall not affect the rights and obligations of any contracting Party deriving from any existing international agreement, except where the exercise of those rights and obligations would cause a serious damage or threat to biological diversity.
2. Contracting Parties shall implement this Convention with respect to the marine environment consistently with the rights and obligations of states under the law of the sea.

23. Conference of the Parties

1. A Conference of the Parties is hereby established. The first meeting of the Conference of the Parties shall be convened by the Executive Director of the United Nations Environment Programme not later than one year after the entry into force of this Convention. Thereafter, ordinary meetings of the Conference of the Parties shall be held at regular intervals to be determined by the Conference at its first meeting.
2. Extraordinary meetings of the Conference of the Parties shall be held at such other times as may be deemed necessary by the conference, or at the written request of any Party, provided that, within six months of the request being communicated to them by the secretariat, it is supported by at least one third of the Parties.
3. The conference of the parties shall by consensus agree upon and adopt rules of procedure for itself and for any subsidiary body it may establish, as well as financial rules governing the funding of the secretariat. At each ordinary meeting, it; shall adopt a budget for the financial period until the next ordinary meeting.
4. The Conference of the Parties shall keep under review the implementation of this convention, and, for this purpose, shall:
   (*a*) Establish the form and the intervals for transmitting the information to be submitted in accordance with Article 26 and consider such information as well as reports submitted by any subsidiary body;
   (*b*) Review scientific, technical and technological advice on biological diversity provided in accordance with Article 25;
   (*c*) Consider and adopt, as required, protocols in accordance with Article 28;

(*d*) Consider and adopt, as required, in accordance with Articles 29 and 30, amendments to this convention and its annexes;

(*e*) Consider amendments to any protocol, as well as to any annexes thereto, and, if so decided, recommend their adoption to the parties to the protocol concerned;

(*f*) Consider and adopt, as required, in accordance with Article 30, additional annexes to this convention;

(*g*) Establish such subsidiary bodies, particularly to provide scientific and technical advice, as are deemed necessary for the implementation of this convention;

(*h*) Contact, through the Secretariat, the executive bodies of conventions dealing with matters covered by this convention with a view to establishing appropriate forms of cooperation with them and

(*i*) Consider and undertake any additional action that may be required for the achievement of the purposes of this Convention in the light of experience gained in its operation.

5. The United Nations, its specialized agencies and the International Atomic Energy Agency, as well as any State not party to this Convention, may be represented as observers at meetings of the Conference of the parties. Any other body or agency, whether governmental or non-governmental, qualified in fields relating to conservation and sustainable use of biological diversity, which has informed the Secretariat of its wish to be represented as an observer at a meeting of the Conference of the Parties, may be admitted unless at least one third of the Parties present object. The admission and participation of observers shall be subject to the rules of procedure adopted by the Conference of the Parties.

24. Secretariat

1. A secretariat is hereby established. Its function shall be:
   (*a*) To arrange for and service meetings of the Conference of the Parties provided for in Article 23;
   (*b*) To perform the Function assigned to it by any protocol;
   (*c*) To Prepared reports on the execution of its functions under this Convention and present them to the conference of the Parties;
   (*d*) To coordinate with other relevant international bodies and, in particular to enter into such administrative and contractual arrangements as may be required for the effective discharge of its functions; and
   (*e*) To perform such other function as may be determined by the Conference of the Parties.
2. At its first ordinary meeting, the Conference of the Parties shall designate the secretariat from amongst those existing competent international organization which have signified their willingness to carry out the secretariat function under this Convention.

25. Subsidiary Body on Scientific Advice

1. A subsidiary body for the provision of scientific, technical and technological advice is hereby established to provide the conference of the parties and, as appropriate, its other subsidiary bodies with timely advice relating to the implementation of this convention. This body shall be open to participation by all parties and shall be multidisciplinary. It shall comprise government representatives competent in the relevant field of expertise. It shall report regularly to the conference of the parties on all aspects o its work.

2. Under the authority of and in accordance with guidelines laid down by the Conference of the Parties and upon its request, this body shall:
   (*a*) Provide scientific and technical assessments of the status of biological diversity;
   (*b*) Prepare scientific and technical assessments of the effects of types of measures taken in accordance with the provisions of this Convention;
   (*c*) Identify innovative, efficient and state-of-the-art technologies and know-how relating to the conservation and sustainable use of biological diversity and advise on the ways and means of promoting development and/or transferring such technologies;
   (*d*) Provide advice on scientific programmes and international cooperation in research and development related to conservation and sustainable use of biological diversity; and
   (*e*) Respond to scientific, technical, technological and methodological questions that the Conference of the Parties and its subsidiary bodies may put to the body.
3. The functions, terms of reference, organization and operation of this body may be further elaborated by the Conference of the Parties.

26. Reports

Each contracting party shall, at intervals to be determined by the Conference of the Parties, present to the Conference of the Parties, reports on measures which it has taken for the implementation of trhe provisions of this convention and their effectiveness in meeting the objectives of this convention.

27. Settlement of Disputes

1. In the event of a dispute between Contracting Parties concerning the interpretation or application of this Convention, the parties concerned shall seeks

solution by negotiation.

2. If the parties concerned cannot reach agreement by negotiation, they may jointly seek the good office of, or request mediation by, a third party.
3. When ratifying, accepting, approving or acceding to this Convention or at any time thereafter, a state or regional economic integration organization may declare in writing to the Depositary that for a dispute not resolved in accordance with paragraph 1 or paragraph 2 above, it accepts one or both of the following means of dispute settlement as compulsory:
   (*a*) Arbitration in accordance with the procedure laid down in part 1 of annex II;
   (*b*) Submission of the dispute to the International Court of Justice.
4. If the parties to the dispute have not, in accordance with paragraph 2 above, accepted the same or any procedure, the dispute shall be submitted to conciliation in accordance with Part 2 of Annex II unless the parties otherwise agree.
5. The provisions of this Article shall apply with respect to any protocol except as otherwise provided in the protocol concerned.

28. Adoption of Protocols

1. The Contracting Parties shall cooperate in the formulation and adoption of protocols to this Convention.
2. Protocols shall be adopted at a meeting of the Conference of the Parties.
3. The text of any proposed protocol shall be communicated to the Contracting Parties by the Secretariat at least six months before such a meeting.

29. Amendment of the Convention or Protocols

1. Amendments to this Convention may be proposed by any Contracting Party. Amendments to any protocol may be proposed by any party to that protocol.

2. Amendments to this Convention shall be adopted at a meeting of the Conference of the parties. Amendments to any protocol shall be adopted at a meeting of the parties to the protocol in question The text of any proposed amendment to this Convention or to any protocol, except as may otherwise be Provide in such protocol, shall be communicated at least six months before the meeting at which it is proposed for adoption. The secretariat shall also communicate proposed amendments to the signatories to this Convention for information.
3. The Parties shall make every effort to reach agreement on any proposed amendment to this Convention or to any protocol by consensus. If all efforts at consensus have been exhausted, and no agreement reached, the amendment shall as a last resort be adopted by a two-third majority vote of the Parties to the instrument in question present and voting at the meeting, and shall be submitted by the Depositary to all parties for ratification, acceptance or approval.
4. Ratification, acceptance or approval of amendments shall be notified to the Depositary in writing. amendments adopted in accordance with paragraph 3 above shall enter into force among parties having accepted them on the ninetieth day after the deposit of instruments of ratification, acceptance or approval by at least two third of the contracting parties to this convention or of the parties to the protocol concerned, except as may otherwise be provided in such protocol. Thereafter the amendments shall enter into force for any other party on the ninetieth day after that party deposits its instrument of ratification, acceptance or approval of the amendments.
5. For the purposes of this Article, "Parties present and voting" means parties present and casting an affirmative or negative vote.

30. Adoption and Amendment of Annexes

1. The annexes to this Convention or to any protocol shall form an integral part of the Convention or to any protocol shall form an integral part of the convention or of such protocol, as the case may be, and, unless expressly provided otherwise, a reference to this convention or its protocols constitutes at the same time a reference to any annexes thereto. Such annexes shall be retracted to procedural, scientific, technical and administrative matters.
2. Except as may be otherwise provided in any protocol with respect to its annexes, the following procedure shall apply to the proposal, adoption and entry into force of additional annexes to this convention or of annexes to any protocol:
   (*a*) Annexes to this Convention or to any protocol shall be proposed and adopted according to the procedure laid down in Article 29;
   (*b*) Any party that is unable to approve an additional annex to this convention or an annex to any protocol to which it is party shall so notify the Depositary, in writing, within one year from the date of the communication of the adoption by the Depositary. The Depositary shall without delay notify all Parties of any such notification received. A Party may at any time withdraw a previous declaration of objection an the annexes shall thereupon enter into force for that party subject to subparagraph (c) below;
   (*c*) On the expiry of one year from the date of the communication of the adoption by the Depositary, the annex shall enter into force for all parties to this convention or to any protocol concerned which have not submitted a notification in accordance with the provisions of subparagraph (b) above.
3. The proposal, adoption and entry into force of

amendments to annexes to this convention or to any protocol shall be subject to the same procedure as for the proposal, adoption and entry into force of annexes to the convention or annexes to any protocol.

4. If an additional annex or an amendment to an annex is related to an amendment to this convention or to any protocol, the additional annex or amendment shall not enter into force until such time amendment to the convention or to the protocol concerned enters into force.

31. Right to Vote

1. Except as provided for in paragraph 2 below, each Contracting Party to this convention or to any protocol shall have one vote.
2. Regional economic integration organizations, in matters within their competence, shall exercise their right to vote with a number of votes equal to the number of their member States which are Contracting Parties to this Convention or the relevant protocol. Such organization shall not exercise their right to vote if their member states exercise theirs, and vice versa.

32. Relationship between this Convention

1. A State or a regional economic integration organization may not become a party to a protocol unless it is, or becomes at the same time, a Contracting party to this convention.
2. Decisions under any protocol shall be taken only by the parties to the protocol concerned. Any contracting Party that has not ratified, accepted or approved a protocol may participate as an observer in any meeting of the parties to the protocol.

33. Signature

This convention shall be open for signature at Rio-de- Janeiro by all states and any regional economic integration organisation from 5th June 1992 until 14th June 1992, and at the United Nations Head Quarters in New York from 15th June 1992 to 4th June 1993.

34. Ratification, Acceptance or Approval

1. This Convention and any protocol shall be subjected to ratification, acceptance or approval by states and by regional economic integration organisations. Instruments of ratification, acceptance or approval shall be deposited with the Depositary.
2. Any organisation referred to in paragraph I above which becomes a contracting party to this convention or any protocol without any of its member states being a contracting party shall be bound by all the obligations under the convention or the protocol, as the case may be. In the case of such organisations, one or more of whose member states is a contracting party to this convention or the relevant protocol, the organisation and its member states shall decide on their respective responsibilities for the peformance of their obligations under the Convention and protocol, as the case may be. In such case, the organisation and the member states shall not be entitled to exercise rights under the Convention or relevant protocol concurrently.
2. In their instruments of ratification, acceptance or approval, the organisations referred to in paragraph 1 above shall declare the extent of their competance with respect to the matter governed by the Convention or the relevant protocol. These organisations shall also inform the Depository of any relevant modification in the extent of their competance.

35. Accession

1. This Convention and any protocol shall be open for accession by States and by regional economic integration organisations from the date on which the

Convention or the protocol concerned is closed for signature. The instruments of accession shall be deposited with the Depositary.

2. In their instruments of accession, the organisations referred to in paragraph 1 above shall declare the extent of their competance with respect to the matters governed by the Convention or the relevant protocol. This organisation shall also inform the Depository of any relevant modification in the extent of their competence.
3. The provision of Article 34, paragraph 2, shall apply to regional economic integration organisations, which accede to this Convention or any protocol.

36. Entry into Force

1. This Convention shall enter into force on the ninetieth day after the date of deposit of the thirtieth instrument of ratification, accetance, approval or accession.
2. Any protocol shall enter into force on the ninetieth day after the date of deposit of the number of instruments of ratification, acceptance, approval or accession, specified in the protocol, has been deposited.
3. For each contracting Party, which ratifies, accepts or approves this Convention or accedes there to after the deposit of the thirtieth instrument of ratification, acceptance, approval or accession, it shall enter into force on the ninetieth day after the date of deposit by such contraction party of its instrument of ratification, acceptance, approval or accession.
4. Any protocol, excepts as otherwise provided in such protocol, shall enter into force for a contracting party that ratifies, accepts or approves that protocol or accedes thereto after its entry into force pursuant to paragraph2 above, on the ninetieth day after the date on which that contracting party deposits its instrument of ratification, acceptance, approval or accession, or on the date on which this convention enters into force for that contracting party.

5. For the purposes of paragraph 1 and 2 above, any instrument deposited by a regional economic integration organization shall not be counted as additional to those deposited by member states of such organization.

37. Reservation

No reservation may be made to this Convention.

38. Withdrawals

1. At any time after two years from the date on which this convention has entered into force for a contracting party, that Contracting party may withdraw from the Convention by giving written notification to the Depositary.
2. Any such withdrawal shall take place upon expiry of one year after the date of its receipt by the Depositary, or on such later date as may be specified in the notification of the withdrawal.
3. Any Contracting party, which withdraws from this convention, shall be considered as also having withdraw from any protocol to which it is party.

39. Financial Interim Arrangements

Provided that it has been fully restructured in accordance with the requirements of Article 21, the Global Environment Facility (GEF) of the United Nations Development Programme, the United Nations Environment Programme and the International Bank for Reconstruction and Development shall be the institutional structure referred to in Article 21 on interim basis, for the period between the entry into force of this convention and the first meeting of the conference of the parties or until the conference of the parties decides which institutional structure will be designated in accordance with Article 21.

40. Secretariat Interim Arrangements

The secretariat to be provided by the Executive Director

of the United Nations Environment Programme shall be the secretariat referred to in Article 24, Paragraph 2, on an interim basis for the period between the entry into force of this convention and the first meeting of the conference of the Parties.

41. Depositary

The secretary-General of the United Nations shall assume the function of Depositary of this Convention and any protocols.

42. Authentic Texts

The original of this Convention, of which the Arabic, Chinese, English, French, Russian and Spanish texts are equally authentic, shall be deposited with the Secretary-General of the United Nations.

IN WITNESS WHERE OF the undersigned, being duly authorized to that effect, have signed this Convention.

Done at Rio-de-Janeiro on this fifth day of June, one thousand nine hundred and ninety-two.

Salient Features of Convention

The 23 preambular paragraphs of the Convention on Biological Diversity recognise and reaffirm:

- the intrinsic value of biological diversity;
- the sovereign rights of State over their biological resources;
- the fundamental requirement of in situ conservation of ecosystems and natural habitats;
- the supporting role of ex situ measures;
- the vital role of local communities and women in the conservation and sustainable use of biological diversity;
- the desirability of sharing equitably the benifits arising from the use of traditional knowledge, skills, innovations and practices;
- the importance of and need to promote regional and

global cooperation for conservation; and
- the requirement of sustainable investments to conserve biological diversity;

Through its 42 Articles, the Convention, by recognising national sovereignty over biological resources calls for facilitation of access to genetic resources on mutually agreed terms and with prior informed consent of the country providing these, with a commitment on the recipient country to share in the benefits of utilising the resources thus provided.

The Convention also calls for the transfer of relevant technologies, including biotechnology, on fair and most favourable terms, from the developed to the developing nations, who mainly are the providers of genetic resources. It also calls on the private sector to facilitate access to and transfer of such technologies developed by them. The contracting parties are to cooperate in this regard to ensure that patents and other intellectual property rights are supportive of and do not run counter to the objective of the convention. The convention commits the parties to consider an international protocol for safe transfer, handling and use of any living, modified organism resulting from biotechnology. The parties are also to take measures for facilitating access on a fair and equitable basis, on mutually agreed terms, to the results and benefits arising from biotechnologies based upon genetic resources transferred. The developed country Parties are committed to contribute to a fund to enable Developing Country Parties to meet the agreed full incremental costs for implementing the provisions of the convention. This financial mechanism is to operate within a democratic and transperent system of governance and function under the authority of the Conference of Parties.

CONFERENCE OF THE PARTIES (COP)

The conference of the Parties is the governing body of the Convention, and advances implementation of the Convention through the decisions it takes at the periodic meetings. The Conference of Parties has held 6 meetings and one extra ordinary meeting since it first met at Nassau, Bahamas in 1994. During 1994 -96 the Conference of Parties held its ordinary meetings annually, but now following a change in procedure in 2000 these meetings will be held in every two years. In its 6 ordinary and one extraordinary meeting the COP has taken a total of 146 procedural and substantive decisions.

The 7th ordinary meting of the Conference of Parties to the Convention on Biological Diversity will be held in Qualalampur, Malaysia from 9 to 20 February, 2004. A brief summary of the previous 6 ordinary meetings with their themes has been given below:

COP 1: First ordinary meeting of the Conference of Parties to the Convention on Biological Diversity was held in Nassau, Bahamas during 28th November to 9th December, 1994. Guidance to financial mechanism and medium term programme of work were the major themes.

COP 2: It was held in Jakarta, Indonesia from 6 to 17 November 1995 with marine and coastal biodiversity, access to genetic resources, conservation and sustainable use of biological diversity and biosafety being the major themes.

COP 3: Third ordinary meeting of COP was held in Buenos Aires, Argentina during 4 to 15 November 1996. The major themes of the meeting were agricultural biodiversity; financial resources and mechanism; identification, monitoring and assessment; intellectual property rights.

COP 4: Held during 4 to 15 May, 1998 at Brastislava, Slovak Republic. Inland water ecosystems; review of the operation of the Convention; article 8(j) and related issues; benefit sharing were the major themes of this meeting.

COP 5: The fifth COP was held in Nairobi, Kenya from 15th to 26th May, 2000. Dryland, Mediterranean, arid, semi arid, grassland and savana ecosystems; sustainable use including tourism and access to genetic resources were the major themes.

COP 6: Held at The Hague, The Neatherlands from 7th to 19th April, 2002. Forest ecosystems; alien species, benefit sharing and strategic plan 2002-2010 were the major themes.

The first Extra Ordinary Meeting of the Conference of Parties to the Convention on Biological Diversity was held in the cities of Cartagena in Colombia during 22-23 February, 1999 and in Montreal, Canada during 24-28 January 2000.

FUTURE PERCEPTION OF BIODIVERSITY

The only biodiversity that may stay stable is the diversity of a species at the gene-level. Again this gets limited by the selective retention and/or cultivation of the desired genotypes needed by the humans and the elimination of the others not needed by humans. Therefore, the quantitative and qualitative components of the living organisms in an area, region, country and continent are never stable or static but are changing too fast; the change is proportional to human activities and influences. Hence, the estimation and quantification of biodiversity of an area may be reliable at genic and genotypic level for a specific span of time. This narrows the concept of biodiversity from the general to the specific level, from the ecosystem to the gene component level or from the overall macro-biodiversity to the micro-biodiversity level. The micro-biodiversity takes into account the genotypic diversity, the environmental variability and the genotype-environmental interactions. These three-tier variability component, comple-ment each other and lead to the stability of biodiversity in an area. Because of the stability, the assessment and evaluation becomes reliable and purposeful for characterising biodiversity of an area.

The exorbitantly high biodiversity in microsatellites arises either by replication slippage or by random DNA recombination process or by both. Since no two individuals have the same genetic profile, because each human has a different set of microsatellite alleles, specific and unique to each individual, the highest biodiversity in the world therefore exists in the microsatellite alleles (M-allel) and its limits form the present day size of the human population over the globe. As the human population is growing fast, the m-allele biodiversity is proportionately enlarging. Does this m-allele biodiversity have an adaptive role or evolutionary significance, is not known. Why does *Homo sapiens* exhibit the highest biodiversity in number, types and forms of different genes in its genome is not known? Surely, the biodiversity in human genome should have a definite role in evolution, adaptation, and survival of humans over this globe.

THE GLOBAL BIODIVERSITY CHALLENGE

A meeting on 2010- The Global Biodiversity Challenge was held in London during 21 to 23 May, 2003, which also coincided with the International Day for Biological Diversity. The Secretariate of the Convention convened this meeting on Biological Diversity in association with the World Conservation Monitoring Centre of the United Nations Environment Programme (UNEP-WCMC) and United Nations Development Programme. Approximately approximately 150 delegates who also included government nominated experts attended this meeting and representatives of biodiversity related conventions, Un agencies, acadenmic and research institutions and other international and national relevant governmental and non-governmental organisations.

9

Environmental Difficulties in Developing Countries

The Intergovernmental Panel on Climate Change (IPCC) recently released a report that claims that the world's poorest populations will be the hardest hit by climate changes (IPCC 2001). The relationship between poverty and climate impacts has been known for some time - and poverty has often been connected to a lack of capacity to adapt to climatic changes (Adger & Kelly 2000). Moreover, poor people often live in risk-filled environments and subsist on natural resources that are negatively affected by climate changes (Kates & Haarman 1992, Blaikie et al. 1994). The IPCC's new emphasis on the poverty issue represents a fundamental shift in focus from climate impacts as a purely natural scientific phenomenon to climate impacts as a development issue. This shift has important consequences for the design and implementation of climate measures.

Climate impacts and development issues

Traditionally, climate has been seen as a global environmental issue, while poverty has been perceived as a local development issue. Thus there may be an initial contradiction between basing climate measures on international environmental agreements, such as the Climate Convention (UNFCCC), and taking poverty issues into account in these measures. Commitments, funding mechanisms, and policy measures established in the wake of climate agreements have been designed from the perspective of climate as a global environmental problem. Generally, a top-down approach to resolving climate issues, rather than a bottom-up approach has been taken. Some critics believe that perceiving environmental problems as global and designing global frameworks to address them implies a form of globalization that represents a new type of imperialism - one where the North gains control over natural resources and steers the development in the South under the guise of global environmental considerations (Mater 1999).

Much of research into development issues represents the second basic view, namely that poverty is a development problem where the best solutions are shaped through local participation and policy measures are adapted to local conditions. In other words, this research takes a bottom-up approach to the problem, even though some of the basic causes of poverty can be global (Chambers 1983). In terms of environmental research, there has been an increasing focus on the interrelationship between environment and development, and how nature and society affect each other through a complex interplay (Boudie 1993, Leach & Mearns 1996, Smith & O'Keefe 1996). This approach also implies that global environmental changes can have very different impacts on different local communities. The IPCC's suggestion that poverty plays an important role in determining how climate changes will affect various populations has two important consequences for policy design principles:

i) That those who are most vulnerable to the impacts of climate change should be the primary target of mitigation policy; poverty issues should be taken into account as a central element in climate measures.

ii) Consequence is that policy design must take into account that the impacts of climate changes and possible effective measures to reduce vulnerability vary both from place to place and from time to time because social conditions change.

It will be just as important to identify how adaptability can be improved among various social groups, as it will be to identify physical climate impacts. Measures should therefore be prepared in cooperation with the local population, where their priorities and conception of the problems become the center of focus.

Local interactions between various environmental problems

An important aspect of local adaptability to environmental change is the interaction between various environmental problems at a local level. To an impoverished farmer, the degradation of several natural resources that together form his or her subsistence base is considered a single problem, even though the causes of the degradation are considered to be separate phenomena at a global level. Environmental problems that are addressed separately at an international level - such as climate, biodiversity, and desertification - must at be tackled holistically at the local level. There are several practical examples of the interaction between several "different" environmental issues in locally adapted measures. One study in two arid agricultural areas (one in the Kitui district in Kenya and the other in the Same district in Tanzania) shows that biodiversity in the form of local tree and plant species distributed throughout the farms represents an alternative income source for poor farmers when crops fail. For example, local wood is used to make stools, kitchen equipment, chicken coops, and so on. These products are sold on the local markets. Lumber is also used to burn charcoal, which is sold to urban areas and cities. Leaves and seeds from certain trees are used as feed for goats and cattle. Drought resistant indigenous fruits are an important source of nutrition for both children and adults when there is little food. Thus preservation of local knowledge and biodiversity in cultivated areas helps enhance adaptability and reduce vulnerability to extreme climate events such as drought and flooding (Eriksen 2000). Preservation of the natural vegetation is also useful in combating desertification. Moreover, particular ridges and hills covered with natural vegetation in dry areas have great value with respect to biodiversity. These areas often have different compositions of plant and animal species that otherwise are not found in the surrounding lowlands (Gachathi 1995). These ridges, which have higher precipitation than the lowlands, form important parts of local watersheds. In addition, there is a better microclimate (local temperatures and moisture) around these forested areas, particularly in arid regions that are dependent on the forests as water sources. Where ridge vegetation is well preserved, forest streams will often be active also during the dry season (Eriksen et al.).

A similar case of where climate and biodiversity measures have been coordinated is in the northern coast of Vietnam and described by Nguyen Hoang Tri and colleagues (1998). Preservation of the natural mangrove forest with its species diversity is important for local sources of income, for example, wood and honey production. The mangrove forest is equally important for protection from cyclones and typhoons. The coast is hit by between one and twelve typhoons per year, and there is great uncertainty about how the frequency and magnitude of these will be changed in connection with global warming. The mangrove forest protects agriculture against flood damage from cyclones and reduces the maintenance costs of the dikes. Preservation of this forest represents a type of climate adaptation.

Measures under the Climate Convention

The Climate Convention requires developing countries to adapt public policy, government, and legislation to accommodate climate measures, both to reduce emissions of greenhouse gases and to adapt to possible climate changes. The Climate Convention from 1992 and the Kyoto Protocol from 1997 have two mechanisms that are particularly relevant with respect to implementing measures directed at developing countries. The Global Environment Facility (GEF) is the Climate Convention's funding scheme, designed to assist developing countries in developing climate strategies and integrating climate considerations into public policy, government, and development plans. The GEF is also supposed to fund preparation and implementation of practical measures, but until now no such GEF supported projects have been implemented. Most of the GEF's financial assistance has been directed at greenhouse gas emissions rather than enhancing local adaptation to climate impacts. As the poorest populations are responsible for very low greenhouse gas emissions but are nevertheless the most vulnerable to possible climate changes, it is thus a challenge to adapt the GEF to support measures designed to assist the poor. To truly integrate poverty considerations - which, for example, can be connected to local property rights - into environmental measures is also a great challenge because the GEF is essentially not a development fund but rather an environment fund. The GEF was established to fund measures specially directed at biodiversity and climate, and development measures are defined as outside its mandate.

The Kyoto Protocol's Clean Development Mechanism (CDM) is another important mechanism to finance measures in developing countries. This mechanism is designed to enable industrialized countries to meet their commitments to the Kyoto Protocol by financing development projects that reduce emissions of greenhouse gases in a developing country. Negotiations are still ongoing with respect to the regulatory framework of the CDM, but pilot projects have already been implemented. It is important that the CDM provide feasible solutions that benefit poor developing countries and that the CDM projects are not designed on the premises of the industrialized countries in a top-down fashion.

Another important source of funding for environmental measures in developing countries is development aid organizations such as NORAD or the World Bank. Since climate issues have previously only minimally been seen as an important development issue, only a few such organizations have paid attention to climate impacts. It will therefore be a challenge both to increase the awareness of the climate issue among these organizations and to enhance the cooperation between these organizations and the UN system in the design of policy measures. This is particularly important because development organizations have valuable experience with how locally adapted measures can be implemented to reach the poorest populations. The focus on poverty and local development is an important step forward in combating the negative impacts of climate change, but at the same time presents tremendous practical challenges. The question is how meaningful local solutions can be found to global problems.

Global Environmental Problems

Trees and wild plants proviTe impoverished farmers in Kenya and Tanzania an alternative subsistence base in times of drought. These kind of local interactions tend to be ignored when climate changes are discussed at the global level.

The Intergovernmental Panel on Climate Change (IPCC) recently released a report that claims that the world's poorest populations will be the hardest hit by climate changes (IPCC 2001). The relationship between poverty and climate impacts has been known for some time - and poverty has often been connected to a lack of capacity to adapt to climatic changes (Adger & Kelly 2000). Moreover, poor people often live in risk-filled environments and subsist on natural resources that are negatively affected by climate changes (Kates & Haarman 1992, Blaikie et al. 1994). The IPCC's new emphasis on the poverty issue represents a fundamental shift in focus from climate impacts as a purely natural scientific phenomenon to climate impacts as a development issue. This shift has important consequences for the design and implementation of climate measures.

The planet is over-populated and its limited resources, unevenly distributed among the world's people, are being used at an accelerated pace. The implications of man's violence to the environment are serious throughout the world and particularly in less developed countries such as India. Air, water, land, and noise pollution constantly imperil quality of life and must be controlled and managed with all the skill at our disposal if man and his environment are to survive.

Climate impacts and development issues

Traditionally, climate has been seen as a global environ-mental issue, while poverty has been perceived as a local development issue. Thus there may be an initial contradiction between basing climate measures on international environ-mental agreements, such as the Climate Convention (UNFCCC), and taking poverty issues into account in these measures. Commitments, funding mechanisms, and policy measures established in the wake of climate agreements have been designed from the perspective of climate as a global environmental problem. Generally, a top-down approach to resolving climate issues, rather than a bottom-up approach has been taken. Some critics believe that perceiving environmental problems as global and designing global frameworks to address them implies a form of globalization that represents a new type of imperialism - one where the North gains control over natural resources and steers the development in the South under the guise of global environmental considerations (Mater 1999). Much of research into development issues represents the second basic view, namely that poverty is a development problem where the best solutions are shaped through local participation and policy measures are adapted to local conditions. In other words, this research takes a bottom-up approach to the problem, even though some of the basic causes of Siri Eriksen Cicerone 2/2001

Global environmental problems and local poverty

Poverty can be global (Chambers 1983). In terms of environ-mental research, there has been an increasing focus on the interrelationship between environment and development, and how nature and society affect each other through a complex interplay (Boudie 1993, Leach & Mearns 1996, Smith & O'Keefe 1996). This approach also implies that global environmental changes can have very different impacts on different local communities. Conservation of the baobab tree (Adansonia digitata) on cultivated land represents one climate adaptation in arid regions in East Africa. The fruit is a useful source of nutrition during drought years. The IPCC's suggestion that poverty plays an important role in determining how climate changes will affect various populations has two important consequences for policy design principles: The first is that those who are most vulnerable to the impacts of climate change should be the primary target of mitigation policy; poverty issues should be taken into account as a central element in climate measures. The second consequence is that policy design must take into account that the impacts of climate changes and possible effective measures to reduce vulnerability vary both from place to place and from time to time because social conditions change. It will be just as important to identify how adaptability can be improved among various social groups, as it will be to identify physical climate impacts. Measures should therefore be prepared in cooperation with the local population, where their priorities and conception of the problems become the center of focus.

Single problem, even though the causes of the degradation are considered to be separate phenomena at a global level. Environmental problems that are addressed separately at an international level - such as climate, biodiversity, and deserti-fication - must at be tackled holistically at the local level. There are several practical examples of the interaction between several "different" environmental issues in locally adapted measures. One study in two arid agricultural areas (one in the Kitui district in Kenya and the other in the Same district in Tanzania) shows that biodiversity in the form of local tree and plant species distributed throughout the farms represents an alternative income source for poor farmers when crops fail. For example, local wood is used to make stools, kitchen equipment, chicken coops, and so on. These products are sold on the local markets. Lumber is also used to burn charcoal, which is sold to urban areas and cities. Leaves and seeds from certain trees are used as feed for goats and cattle. Drought resistant indigenous fruits are an important source of nutrition for both children and adults when there is little food. Thus preservation of local knowledge and biodiversity in cultivated areas helps enhance adaptability and reduce vulnerability to extreme climate events such as drought and flooding (Eriksen 2000). Preservation of the natural vegetation is also useful in combating desertification.

Moreover, particular ridges and hills covered with natural vegetation in dry areas have great value with respect to biodiversity. These areas often have different compositions of plant and animal species that otherwise are not found in the surrounding lowlands (Gachathi 1995). These ridges, which have higher precipitation than the lowlands, form important parts of local watersheds. In addition, there is a better microclimate (local temperatures and moisture) around these forested areas, particularly in arid regions that are dependent on the forests as water sources. Where ridge vegetation is well preserved, forest streams will often be active also during the dry season (Eriksen et al.).

A similar case of where climate and biodiversity measures have been coordinated is in the northern coast of Vietnam and described by Nguyen Hoang Tri and colleagues (1998). Preservation of the natural mangrove forest with its species diversity is important for local sources of income, for example, wood and honey production. The mangrove forest is equally important for protection from cyclones and typhoons. The coast is hit by between one and twelve typhoons per year, and there is great uncertainty about how the frequency and magnitude of these will be changed in connection with global warming. The mangrove forest protects agriculture against flood damage from cyclones and reduces the maintenance costs of the dikes. Preservation of this forest represents a type of climate adaptation. These examples illustrate that the interaction between various "global" environmental problems can result in different impacts in different places. To reduce the vulnerability of the poorest populations, policy measures should be adapted to local conditions, and address several different environmental problems at the same time.

In developing countries seeking to expand their economic activities, consideration for environmental conservation often receives a low priority. In addition, approaches used in industria-lized countries often cannot be applied directly in developing countries. In this context, NIES is conducting research on ways to conserve the environment that are appropriate for developing country conditions.

Water quality and air pollution are serious problems in developing countries in the Asian region. Air pollution in major cities marked by many factories and heavy vehicle traffic also has high concentrations of sulfur dioxide and suspended particulate matter (SPM), at levels Japan experienced in the past. In addition, problems such as damage from acid rain and transboundary pollution are growing more serious. Pollution of rivers and lakes from chemical substances (including agricultural chemicals) and eutrophication (including abnormal growth of toxic algae) are also occurring more frequently, while water shortages and tropical forest destruction are worsening.

While many developing countries give economic development the greatest priority, many problems remain with basic needs such as safe drinking water and food, as well as medical and public health services. This situation often hinders progress in addressing environmental problems. In some countries, including Bangladesh, China and India, negative health impacts are growing over large areas due to fluorine and arsenic pollution in air and drinking water implementing measures directed at developing countries. The Global Environment Facility (GEF) is the Climate Convention's funding scheme, designed to assist developing countries in developing climate strategies and integrating climate considerations into public policy, government, and development plans. The GEF is also supposed to fund preparation and implementation of practical measures, but until now no such GEF supported projects have been implemented. Most of the GEF's financial assistance has been directed at greenhouse gas emissions rather than enhancing local adaptation to climate impacts. As the poorest populations are responsible for very low greenhouse gas emissions but are nevertheless the most vulnerable to possible climate changes, it is thus a challenge to adapt the GEF to support measures designed to assist the poor. To truly integrate poverty considerations - which, for example, can be connected to local property rights - into environmental measures is also a great challenge because the GEF is essentially not a development fund but rather an environment fund. The GEF was established to fund measures specially directed at biodiversity and climate, and development measures are defined as outside its mandate.

The Kyoto Protocol's Clean Development Mechanism (CDM) is another important mechanism to finance measures in developing countries. This mechanism is designed to enable industrialized countries to meet their commitments to the Kyoto Protocol by financing development projects that reduce emissions of greenhouse gases in a developing country. Negotiations are still ongoing with respect to the regulatory framework of the CDM, but pilot projects have already been implemented. It is important that the CDM provide feasible solutions that benefit poor developing countries and that the CDM projects are not designed on the premises of the industrialized countries in a top-down fashion. Another important source of funding for environmental measures in developing countries is development aid organizations such as NORAD or the World Bank. Since climate issues have previously only minimally been seen as an important development issue, only a few such organizations have paid attention to climate impacts. It will therefore be a challenge both to increase the awareness of the climate issue among these organizations and to enhance the cooperation between these organizations and the UN system in the design of policy measures. This is particularly important because development organizations have valuable experience with how locally adapted measures can be implemented to reach the poorest populations. The focus on poverty and local development is an important step forward in combating the negative impacts of climate change, but at the same time presents tremendous practical challenges. The question is how meaningful local solutions can be found to global problcms.

For a long time man has assumed that the environment enveloping his existence was in vulnerable, bountiful, and immense in its capacity to support life. Events of the last two centuries have belied these presuppositions. The exuberance of the new era of technology and abundance has evaporated and the bright prospects of economic progress and superabundant living have been shattered by the discovery of the finiteness of the planet. With all the technological developments, the world still suffers from the scourges of poverty, disease, and misery, along with environmental degradation, destruction of forests, and extinction of many species. The basic fact of this planet is that it is overpopulated. An increasing number of people are becoming urbanized, they continue to consume resources for survival, and to utilize them at an accelerated pace. By the end of the century, the population will swell to about 6.5 billion, two-thirds of whom will be living in developing countries. The prospect of supporting such a vast human population on the planet seems stupendous and grim, making the future of man unpredictable. It is now clearly recognized that urban man is continuously destroying many useful elements of life by using them indiscriminately and, consequently, degrading the environment which sustains life. It has been scientifically established that the ecosystem of the Spaceship Earth is fragile, limited, and that man's tampering with it may, in the end, make the earth unlivable, not only for man but for all life forms. Man has begun to live in large agglomerations of millions of people; he has command of technologies, which can take him to the farthest planets in the solar system; and he has unraveled mysteries that were secrets of nature only 100 years ago. In a sense, the twentieth century could have been a turning point in man's consciousness about himself and his universe, which should have freed the human race from the perennial threats of destitution, privation, and death. In reality, however, urban life in many parts of the world has become an insult to mankind because of the total degradation of people and their environment. In this context, UNESCO's "Man and the Biosphere Program" (MAB) states its objective to be "development of a basis through natural and social sciences for the rational use and conservation of the resources of the biosphere and improvement of the relation between man and the environment." Further, it states that "the consequences of today's actions on tomorrow's world should be predicted and man must manage natural resources efficiently." This report succinctly underscores the uncertain future of man if the symbiotic relationship between man and his environment continues to deteriorate at the present rate.

All through the two million years of man's existence on the planet, his survival has been conditioned by the intricate balance among the various elements of the earth, which have provided a continuous supply of materials for his needs. During the last 300 years, how ever, man's relationship with the earth, its environment, and outer space has changed drastically be cause of the accumulation of vast knowledge, increasing technology, exponential increase in expectations and needs, and, finally, a quantum jump in human activities by exploding population.

The techno logical revolution has ushered in a new era of transformation, which has not left any part of, the biosphere untouched, directly or indirectly, making man's survival increasingly precarious. Urbanization, as well, has resulted in a new order of relationships between human society and the ecosystem. The Earth went through a series of drastic changes for billions of years until, ultimFtely, life originated, leading eventually to the evolution of man. Only recently, the complex web of human activities has generated extensive modifications of the environment. Every moment man is displacing millions of tons of various elements from one area to another, trans-forming them from one form to another, and converting them into a. large number of products through different processes. For example, 800 million tons of various metals are taken from the earth, 40 million tons of toxic chemicals, and 7 billion tons of conditional fuel units are consumed every year.

In short, the immense number of industrial activities of man is producing vast quantities of pollutants, which result in massive degradation of the environment. An alarming threat to the life-preserving ecosystem is evident around the globe. It can be observed in acid rains, disappearance of plant and animal species, desertification, smog, destruction of coastal areas, dirty waterways, poisoned foods, and blaring noises. Looking at the plight of the enduring earth, what Barry Commoner once said seems to be true: "We have been living under a vast and potentially fatal illusion: that we can enjoy the enormous benefits of modern technology with out risk to the integrity of human life and the environment." Slowly, land, air, and water are being vandalized by man's vast, indiscriminate plundering of the environment. How far the ecosystem of the earth will be able to bear the threat before collapsing is only a question of time. Exploding population, increasingly complex technology, and careless use of resources have joined to face us with a triple danger. Unless man finds another suitable environment or creates a new one, or unless he adapts to the increasingly polluted environment, he must put the planet in order by restoring natural equilibrium if he does not want to face extinction.

Local interactions between various environmental problems

An important aspect of local adaptability to environmental change is the interaction between various environmental problems at a local level. To an impoverished farmer, the degradation of several natural resources that together form his or her subsistence base is considered a Siri Eriksen Cicerone 2/2001

Population and Resources

One stark reality of the world today is that it carries the weight of 4.6 billion people, two-thirds of who live in technologically less- advanced countries and 30 percent of whom-mostly in developing countries-live in perpetual poverty. About 35 percent of the people live in urban areas, mostly in the Western countries. Despite all the measures to control population, this year alone, 90 million more people will be added to the total population. It is in the context of such a vast population that the question of resources becomes urgent.

For thousands of years, man was not aware of the vast wealth of the earth. With the advances in technology, he discovered a great many resources, giving him a feeling that they were unlimited, abundant enough to last forever. Such euphoria, however, did not last long; and now, in more recent years, it has been clearly recognized that many important materials needed for his development, progress, and survival are becoming scarce each day. Yet the demand and consumption of renewable and nonrenewable resources has been increasing by leaps and bounds.

Many areas of the earth are deforested relentlessly, leading to shortages of lumber, newsprint, and fuel. Despite several attempts to tap new sources of energy, the world suffers from an energy crisis, which is worsening each year. In the coming years the world will face increasing shortages of many important materials. In the less industrialized countries, three phenomena illustrate the stark reality:

1. Population explosion-rate of in crease from 2 to 3.5 percent per year;
2. Slow industrial and technological development-an average industrial growth rate of 2.5 percent;
3. Large-scale poverty-30 percent of the world

population living in total deprivation of the basic needs.

No discussion on environmental problems of developing countries would be adequate without an understanding of these realities, which face the vast majority of people in a hundred countries in Asia, Africa, and South America. The shocking contrast of living conditions with those of the industrialized countries is reflected in low life expectancy, meager water, supply, starvation diet, vast slums, inadequate medical facilities, and the total wretched conditions in which people live. Despite all thc efforts to bridge the gap between the industrialized and the poor countries, it has been widening consistently during the last thirty years and, unless some drastic changes happen in the international economic and political order, there will be two human worlds on the planet by the end of the century.

Many of the developing countries are located near the equator, have a great many natural resources and an abundance of sunlight. Their environmental problems are quite different from those in the industrialized countries. The developing countries are in a hurry to advance technologically while they are poor. Vast stretches of forests are denuded and because of the improper selection of technology, improper planning, and the lack of legal protection, the environment is polluted shamelessly. Some of the cities in developing countries a re environ mentally worse than in the industrialized countries; for example, Karachi is more polluted than Stockholm. It is in the framework of less developed countries that we must examine the environmental - problems of India.

The environment in India

In the subcontinent of India, a large part of humanity is huddled together. The second most populated country in the world, with 635 million people, increasing at the rate of 2 percent a year, it will have approximately 900 million people at the end of the century. Seventy- eight percent of the people live in 560,000 villages and the rest in 4,000 cities and towns. The per capita income of India is approximately $150 per year. India is expected to produce 130 million metric tons of food this year. For centuries a vast majority of Indians have depended on wood and cow dung for energy. Vast areas of India have been deforested through the centuries and there is no abeyance of this process in sight. Simultaneously, with deforestation there has been a continuous danger to the wildlife. Recently, a survey identified that approxi-mately 52 animal species in India are on the endangered list.

More seriously, however, India faces a crisis of clean and potable water supply. In the country as a whole, approximately 60 percent of the people do not get safe water for drinking and, personal hygiene. Recently, a Union Minister said that over 25 percent of the urban population in India does not have safe water and 65 percent do not have a sewage system. It is estimated that the daily average supply of water per person in Delhi, Calcutta, Bombay, and Madras is 180, 140, 130, and 80 liters, respectively. Limited supply, poor quality of water, and waste are some of the major problems affecting urban areas.

In the rural areas the water situation is disgraceful despite the fact that under the Fifth Five-Year Plan it was expected that 90 percent of all villages would be provided with safe drinking water at a cost of Rs 550 crores. * Some time ago, the Central Water and Power Commission said that it would cost India Rs 5800 crores to provide minimum water supply to its rural population and an optimum level of water supply and sewerage facilities to the urban population.

Pollution in India

Rachel L. Carson once said,

> "For the first time in the history of the world, every human being is now subjected to contact with dangerous chemicals, from the moment of conception until death."

Despite the fact that India is a rural country, the endless streams of effluents and poisonous gases discharged by industries, power generators, transportation systems, and other human activities pollute its air, water, and land. Even modern agriculture has aggravated the problem of pollution by supplying nitrogen fertilizers, insecticides, pesticides and herbicides, which are washed off by rains into rivers and the sea.

More seriously, many heavy metals, such as mercury, lead, and cadmium, are found in the waters of the River Ganges and the Arabian Ocean near Bombay. A recent survey of air pollution by the Bombay Municipal Corporation has identified heart and lung diseases, such as asthma, bronchitis, emphysema, and even tuberculosis and cancer, related to the air pollution. Even though it is generally recognized that the urban communities suffer from acute forms of pollution, particularly air pollution and noise pollution, it is quite common to find paper, pulp, and 'sugar factories polluting rivers and streams.

Many chronic diseases such as jaundice, cholera, and gastroenteritis, which are related to the impurities of water, are found in villages and cities all over India. The total social and economic cost of pollution is yet to be measured. Except in the major cities, there is no awareness about the environment or pollution. There is no significant movement to control pollution or improve the environment. On the contrary, many planners, administrators, and policymakers live in an euphoria of arrogance and complacency, assuming that everything is fine with the environment and pollution is either impersonal or an inexorable price of technological progress. Sometimes, it is even charged that pollution is a Western technique for keeping a developing country undeveloped. For some people "poverty is the worst pollution." There is no perceptible conservation movement.

Air pollution

Air and water pollution are the most serious and obvious. By and large, the crisis of air pollution is concentrated in industrial areas. The major air pollutants identified in the cities of India are carbon dioxide, carbon monoxide, particulates, hydrocarbons, sulphur dioxide, and nitrogen oxides, The major sources of air pollution in the urban and industrial areas are industrial processes (40%), transportation (25%), fuel production (25%), others (10%). Industrial processes include cement manufacturing, iron foundries, iron and steel mills, pulp and paper mills, petroleum refineries, phosphate fertilizer plants, coal cleaning, and the smelters of aluminum, copper, lead and zinc. In the city of Bombay alone, air pollution has increased tenfold during the last 25 years. There are approximately 15,000 industries located in the city and 250,000 vehicles.

In the winter months, smog is a major menace in Bombay, Calcutta, Baroda, Durgapur, Ahmedabad, and Poona. In all these cities, CO and SO have been significantly in creasing in recent years. The trend extrapolation of the air pollution level in four major metropolitan cities of India has shown that it will be four times greater than what it is today, unless some drastic measures are taken immediately. Unfortunately, there is no Air Pollution Act in India to date. It is hoped that the Act before the Parliament will be passed soon and the necessary measures taken to control air pollution. It would be helpful if the tree plantation programs in the cities were undertaken soon to aid in cleaning the environment.

Water pollution

Water pollution is equally insidious arid more widespread than air pollution in India. As pointed out earlier, large and small water bodies around the country have become cesspools because of large quantities of effluents discharged indiscriminately. The major industrial offenders are petroleum, chemicals, paper and pulp,and sugar. Another major contributor to water pollution is sewage from cities. Only seven percent of the population in India is covered by drainage systems and only an insignificant amount of sewage is treated.

Development of sewage and drainage facilities has been miserable in most of the urban areas. Out of 4,000 cities and towns, hardly 250 have any sort of sewage system. More than 50 percent of the population in urban areas does not have this basic amenity. It is also well known that most of the coastal areas around Bombay, Calcutta, and other cities are highly polluted. The Fishermen's Association of Bombay pointed out in 1978 that their fish catch had been reduced to hardly 15 percent of what they caught 25 years ago, and most of the time they have to go far out into the sea to get any significant catch. Most of the beaches around Bombay, Calcutta, and Madras are not fit for swimming.

In 1974, the government of India passed the Water Pollution Act, requiring that each state set up water pollution control authorities. Most of these authorities lack funds, trained people, and facilities to implement the Act. Yet, within the last four years significant steps were taken to control water pollution problems in major cities by requiring the industries to set up pollution control measures and treat their effluent. The standards of effluent control are high, and it will require at least five more years before a significant impact on the quality of water will be perceptible. The lack of sewerage and drainage facilities is a serious urban problem. It is estimated that the cost of cleaning rivers and coastal areas of India will be no less than Rs 7,000 crores. There are neither plans nor finances for such a gigantic task. Moreover, it is not realistic to expect a large number of cities and towns to have sewerage facilities when their basic problem is to supply the minimum fresh water.

However, in a warm country like India, many economical and simple methods of sewage treatment-such as oxidation ponds-cap be de signed. In the city of Bombay, plans are underway to dispose of sewage through outfalls, 10 kilometers into the sea. In Ahmedabad, where there is a sewage treatment plant, it is not used. Instead, because of its high quality of nutrients, sewage is utilized for growing grass. Some industries, like Union Carbide, re cycle their effluent. In short, extensive efforts are underway to protect the water bodies from pollution. Like supplying potable water, wastewater treatment is an expensive proposition. With increasing industrialization and large concentration of population in urban areas, not only the need for a water supply has been accelerated, but also the amount of sewage produced has proportionately increased. Rivers and oceans have become receptacles for enormous amounts of industrial waste. It is seldom realized that the water system of the earth is rather fragile and its capacity to recycle and supply fresh water perennially is limited. In fact, several types of effluents have already destroyed marine life and depleted oxygen supply. Some of the poisonous elements even reach people through food chains, thus causing damage to our health. Oceans and rivers cannot be a panacea for liquid and solid waste problems. A scientific system of treating industrial waste is probably the only answer. Extensive re search in this area will open new vistas for the development and protection of water resources.

Noise pollution

Among the various enemies of man, one that is most insidious, disquieting, and dangerous is noise, which menaces a large part of humanity now living as members of industrial urban civilization. Each year an increasing number of people are becoming urbanized; the number of cities is increasing, and their sizes are enlarging. In each city, man is exposed to a larger number of technologies, their products and by products. One poisonous by-product of these technologies is pandemonium, which is becoming pain fully louder each year, and may drive cacophonous urban dwellers to permanent silence. In India the situation is dismally pathetic. Some years ago the National Physical Laboratory conducted studies on traffic noise in major cities of India. The studies revealed that the street noise during the day in cities like Bombay and Delhi was intolerably as high as 90 dB* and it was seldom below 60 dB. Similar conditions exist in many other cities and towns around the country. In a recent survey by the Urban Development Institute, it was observed that Bombay was the noisiest city in the country with the largest number of moving vehicles (250,000). Its average daytime noise level was 75 dB, the highest being 105 dB near the airport. The main island continues to remain noisy even during the night, whereas the noise level in the suburbs begins to subside after 11 p.m. The main city can be called the "Island of Cacophony."

If the noise trends in Bombay continue at the present rate we shall, overall, add one decibel a year and reach a dangerous point by the turn of the century. Of the 7.6 million people living in Bombay, at least 30 percent are affected adversely by noise. Besides hearing impairment, they suffer from various other health hazards, including many minor disruptions such as sleeplessness, communication disturbances, and other ills. The industrial aspects of the life we live create much of the noise, but a great deal of it is the result of improper values and unconcern for the environment.

Unlike the problems of other environmental pollutants, there is sufficient knowledge today to control and abate most sources of noise. Various technological, socio-cultural, educational, and legislative A crore is 10,000,000; thus Rs 550 crore is 5,500,000,000 rupees. A rupee is about $12; there are approximately 8.25 rupees to the American dollar. Measures are required to build a peaceful environment. There is no Noise Pollution Act in India today, yet controlling noise pollution is cheaper than controlling any other pollution.

Land pollution

The generation of solid waste in a developing country like India is quite limited. An average Indian produces 1 pound of garbage per day, compared to an average European who produces 4 pounds per day and an American who produces five pounds per day. Fortunately, urban refuse in the cities .of India is mostly organic, containing very little plastic. Approximately 10,000 people earn their living by collecting papers, metals, and bottles, earning Rs 5-30 a day. The removal of recyclable materials is common all over India. In this sense, India is a highly conserving country. Unfortunately, refilling the land has wasted the remaining solid waste. Recognizing that urban solid waste has a high content of organic materials, only recently a 300-ton plant has been set up in Bombay to compost it. Even though such compost would be 25 percent more expensive than the chemical fertilizers, its value as soil conditioner has been well recognized; and it is hoped that soon many such plants will be set up in major cities of India to use solid waste economically. In the rural areas, villagers always work in the closed-loop system of utilizing their limited solid waste for the purpose of agriculture or energy. During the last 10 years, extensive efforts have been underway to set up gobar gas plants to produce methane gas and use the remaining waste as fertilizer. Already approximately 80,000 such plants have been set up. Even though there is no Act to control solid waste pollution, this problem can be tackled more easily, with out sophisticated technologies, for generating resources.

Recommendation for Pollution Control

It is estimated that by the year 2000 approximately 335 million out of 900 million people in India will be living in about 5,000 urban settlements. Concomitantly, the march of industrialization will continue, resulting in increasing problems of pollution. It is not possible to slow down technological advancement, much less stop it, even in a poor country like India. It is a sine qua non of planetary existence that man is symbiotically related to the earth's environment. While technological development must continue, its mindless recklessness towards the ecosystem must stop. We must check the environmental poisoning. In order to do so, it is imperative that some immediate steps be taken.

Decentralization

The most urgent task is to contain megalopolization of

our cities through a definitive policy of decentralization. Plans should be made for regional development in order to distribute industrialization to various levels of settlements. In this sense, the present arbitrary division between urban and rural development should at once be eliminated, and balanced industrial investments, de pendent upon various socioeconomic and environmental factors, must be encouraged. Many problems of urban pollution in India are due to the extremely high concentration of people in urban areas, generating an abnormal number of industrial and other human activities. Huge economic losses due to smoke, dust, and poor zoning practices, in addition to the creation of blighted areas in cities, are due to disorderly and hap hazard development. The pollution problems in our cities can be at tacked more systematically and effectively only if they are of manages able size. For most people, amorphous and large cities represent ultimate forms of degradation. Hence, we must approach our cities through systems planning, taking into account all aspects of urban life and, more importantly, the human consideration, since cities are built for people and not the other way around.

Industrial pollution control

It is cheaper to prevent pollution at the source than to treat it at the end. Too long, industries and government have taken for granted that pollution is a necessary part of production, and the cost of pollution has been externalized in the form of the price paid by the public through ill health or early deaths. Such externalization of cost must be stopped. Industries must have systematic plans of introducing pollution control technologies in different stages. And for this, if necessary, the government must give various incentives, even to the extent of financial assistance for pollution control. If industries pose serious health hazards to the public in highly concentrated areas, as are posed by the Bombay Gas Company, it is imperative that such industries institute pollution control devices, be moved to safe areas, or even be closed. No industry has a right to play with the health and safety of a large number of people. Municipal Corporations must pre pare a long-range plan in terms of settlements and industrial development in order that high-polluting industries do not become a menace to urban society. If such long-range planning had been done 25 years ago, the Fertilizer Corporation of India plant would not have been put in Chembur. It is important to undertake preoperational surveys to determine the existing levels of contaminants and possible types of pollutants under the existing meteorological conditions before setting up an industrial plant. Recognizing that resources are limited, all efforts should be made to recycle or recover whatever is possible from waste. For example, many plants have been set up in the United States during the last 5 years which pro duce 100 percent recycled papers.

Planning

From the above analysis, it is obvious that demands on the limited resources of the planet are increasing in geometrical progression, due to the fast growing population and their insatiable needs. If the standard of living of an average American is taken as desirable, than hardly half a billion people in the world can survive. Unfortunately, the resources of the world, particularly in a poor country like India, are inequitably distributed; so also is technological development, resulting in a tremendous waste on one hand and deprivation on the other. With all the technological developments, it does not seem possible that even the present population of the earth can be sup ported at the minimum expected level. Yet, the population goes on in creasing unabated. No technology has made a significant impact on this problem. On the other hand, there is a limitation to the resources and their growth, and scarcities are growing relentlessly everywhere, leading to an ever-increasing struggle for them. Some of the perishable resources will be exhausted in time, whereas the renewable resources will remain limited.

Logically, one hopes tc find a solution to resource

scarcity in a technological leap, but that turns out to be illusive at each stage. Side effects of some of the technologies are gross and dangerous, as in the case of the automobile, and the development of pollution-control technologies is rather slow and costly. In these circumstances, one clear alternative is to take stock of what is available and plan growth in a limited fashion. In this respect, it is imperative to include the devastating cost of pollution when computing the cost of technology. Some amount of pollution is necessary as a price or progress; but it cannot be allowed to reach the irreversible level where it destroys the fundamental-life sup porting system on which man has to depend. In a simple sense, planning is a process of mobilizing limited re sources for directed goals in order to optimize development.

Such planning will require the following deliberate efforts:

- Objective assessment of available resources;
- Broad understanding of all the available and possible technologies-their cost, capabilities, and side effects;
- Determination of the optimum population which can be supported within the given system and keeping it at that level until change is warranted;
- Control of all production which is nonessential and wasteful until the basic requirements of the population are met;
- Setting priorities in terms of allocation of resources for accelerated growth and development without any damage to the ecosystem;
- Developing technologies and processes which would assist nature to recycle Resources for multiple utilization;
- Matching human and physical re sources in effective relations in order to optimize the results;
- Exploring new sources of acquiring and producing resources for developmental purposes;

- Identifying future trends concerning man, his demands, resources, and possible technologies; finally,
- Managing man and physical systems efficiently and effectively;

Government

An Environmental Planning Ministry should be established on a national level, with state and municipal subsidiaries. The task of such a ministry or agency should be:

- To collect overall data on environ mental conditions, pollution, and environmental damage to health, as well as on other aspects of human urban life.
- It should have strict legislative authority and the machinery to control all forms of pollution- air, water, noise, and thermal.
- There should be a master plan for total urban develop-ment, which would emphasize scientific and aesthetic environ mental planning.
- The government must support and en courage research in pollution control technologies either through indus-tries or universities or other educational institutes. And, most importantly, such an agency should have the expertise available to guide and advise industries or other agencies on how to control pollution.
- There is no escaping the fact that definite standards and norms must be established and enforced.

Conservation

There should be a total plan for conservation of the environment- beaches, parks, lakes, rivers, and streets. In this regard, we must create a green belt around each city in order to stop the endless sprawl. More than 10 years ago London declared a five- mile green belt, as did Leningrad. India has been continuously deforested. At the present rate of destruction of trees, there may not be any forest by the end of the century. A massive program of creating forests and planting trees should be enunciated immediately. People should even be encouraged to grow plants in their homes. Vast areas around cities like Bombay remain fallow and are not cultivated.

Special efforts should be made to develop large vegetable gardens to supply the city, as is done in Peking and Osaka. Solid waste from the city can be composted and used as fertilizer for these gardens.

Education

Ultimately, environment belongs to the people. If people are apathetic, careless, and callous, no one can protect the environment. The result will be cities that are vast dumps of environmental garbage. The most important lesson to be learned from ecology is respect for the environment. Our urgent task is to inculcate ecological conscience: maintaining a reverence for our surroundings and nature cannot be taken for granted. For this purpose, educational programs must be undertaken through television, films, radio, newspapers, and schools. Such education should teach people not only simple things like where to throw garbage, and how to keep places clean, and why not to make noise, but more importantly to understand legislation and how to use it for the purpose of protecting society. Ultimately, people must develop a sense of beauty and humane environment.

Society

Recognizing that India is a poor country with limited resources and a large number of people, protection of the environment requires immediate limits of exploitation. Population must be controlled immediately: All wasteful use of resources must be discontinued. For example, if 25 percent of the pollution in cities like Bombay is due to automobiles, all our investments must be in public and mass transportation systems in order that the use of private automobiles is reduced or even discontinued. Since resources remain limited, urgent priorities should be set up for their equitable and judicious utilization. There is no other way to bring environmental equilibrium. Society divided between stark poverty on the one hand, created by Malthusian refugees, and reckless waste on the other, generated by Madison Avenue Mandarins, threatens urban man with pollution, sterility, and unstable society Pollution is a disease of environment.

Man has originated and survived because an environmental equilibrium has provided all the ingredients for the realization of his immense potential. This equilibrium cannot be distorted or dismantled without jeopardizing the very survival of man. To assure that survival, society must treat the environment with cooperation and a sense of commitment. This demands sacrifice and may mean a simpler style of life for all-a revolution in thinking to go beyond prestige, power, and profit. The proper utilization of technology for quality of life will release in numerable potentialities of man and nature for his ultimate happiness.

Conclusion

We must recognize that the Space ship Earth and the life on it are delicate, limited, and finite. In the total resource system, water, air, and land play a vital role. The supply of many resources on earth is predetermined and, with increasing demand, it has become scarcer at each stage of industrial development. It is possible to provide the minimum for survival, to every Indian. In a country like India, which is technologically less advanced, such a task is steep, requiring some bold, imaginative, and ruthless measures. If, however, the present trends continue, then the resource crisis will reach a catastrophic proportion by the end of the century, driving half the population of the country to wretchedness and simultaneously destroying the very fabric of the environment, which preserved the civilization for many millennia.

There is an insidious attempt to confuse the issues of poverty and pollution. While pollution in developing countries like India is growing steadily, damaging particularly the poor sections of the society, pollution control technologies developed in industrially advanced countries have achieved benefits through massive environmental cleaning programs supported by vast sums of money. Such is the case in the United States, for example, where according to the Fifth Annual Report of the Council on Environmental Quality, that country will spend $20 billion a year until 1982 for environmental improvement. In India, the pressing need is to bring economic growth through agricul-tural and industrial development, which will also accommodate the increasing population pressure. It is precisely because India is a poor country, and large masses of people in the cities are degraded to squalid conditions, that environ mental degradation becomes a serious threat to development and even survival. While, in our cities, pollution in all forms is increasing exponen-tially, the resources necessary to meet even the basic needs of the people are depleting very fast. The discussion on pollution and poverty boils down to the question of re source generation and resource utilization. Our ingenuity must be used to convert waste into resources. India can and should attack the problems of pollution and poverty simultaneously.

In the end, it must be recognized that the environmental crisis is as real as any disaster. Before the country is turned into a wasteland, we must dispel two illusions; the environment, in the form of air, water, and land is not given to us free; and the technologies have answers to all our problems. We must work out an environmental equation which can give us a picture approximate to Our conditions and, at the same time, point out possibilities for creativity and beauty unknown to man in all the past ages. The ultimate hope of survival for human society depends upon a clean, safe, and healthy environment. To quote Barbara Ward and Rene Dubos:

Alone in space, alone in its life-supporting systems, powered by inconceivable energies, mediating them to us through the most delicate adjustments, wayward, unlikely, un predictable, but nourishing, enlivening and enriching in the largest degree-is this not a precious home for all of us earthlings? Is it not worth our love? Does it not deserve all the inventiveness and courage and generosity of which we are capable to preserve it from degradation and destruction and, by doing so, to se cure our own survival?"

10

Impact of Liberalization on Environment

Introduction

Liberalization of investment and the opening of trade through the free trade agreement signed to date have had severe social and environmental impacts on people and his noosphere. The people of India aspire to an international economy based on different principles - an economy that makes sustainability a priority. The problem with classic trade and investment policy from an environmental perspective is that it "externalizes" (does not account for) environmental and social costs, while fostering more intensive energy use, over-exploitation of natural resources, and damage to biodiversity, all of which erode the underlying basis of the economy and society. Such policies intensify expropriation of genetic resources, the destruction of natural ecosystems, environmental degradation in agricultural and urban areas, environmental deregulation, and the violation of the individual and collective civil rights of present and future generations. Environmental degradation has a disproportionate effect on people living in poverty, as these groups tend to live amidst the contaminated habitats and resources in places where there is less political will to improve conditions. Supporters of these policies view these components of sustainable development as limitations to trade (e.g. food security, the protection of biodiversity, the sustainable use of ecosystems and the fair and equitable ways of sharing the benefits of natural resources). Governments for the most part have rejected these ideals, yielding instead to international market pressures. Environmental concerns cut across all topics. Therefore the points set out below are taken up more concretely or complemented in other chapters, such as those on energy and intellectual property rights.

The environment debate over the last few years, the mass movements against the degrading habitat and enactment of various laws and legislations have forced the industrial sectors at first to adopt an uncertain attitude, denying that the problem really existed, or debating whether or not it was its concern. They subsequently adopted some empirical solutions based on the principle of solving problems as and when they arose and according to the specific demands of each individual case (pollution reclamation etc.) on a short-term basis. Therefore, no coherent strategic framework was devised for a long time to avoid this piecemeal approach because it was most probably thought to be of little practical use or may be they were not mentally prepared to make investment towards environment protection from their total profit margin. The problems were face separately without a wider overall solution in mind. As a consequence several solutions were found to be inadequate because the complexity of the subject was not fully grasped.

In recent times, however, aggravation of certain factors, both intrinsic and extrinsic, have forced them to redefine its future plans regarding environmental measures. Also with tremendous scientific progress in the field of Environment Impact Assessment (EIA) and Environment Management Plan (EMP) precise definitions of the measures to be taken in different aspects of environmental degradation have been grasped theoretically. We call it theoretical because hardly anything was ac ihved in spite of all scientific endeavors, all the environmental enactments and laws and all the mass movements and agitations against degrading habitat.

In India the ecological crisis is not of a nature that can be solved by opening a Department of Environment or by sanctioning more research projects (mostly pretentious) on environmental issues. Bureaucratic solutions to this deep-rooted malaise can only provide cosmetic changes and not long-term solution. Nevertheless, an impression is created that increasing number of files marked "Environment" in our Government offices and research institutes represent an effective attack on ecological front. What is happening on ecological front today is certainly making more jobs and money for the white-collar class, but there is every doubt whether it can be considered as an effective effort for conservation. The greatest shortcomings of the present day "environment management programme" are their fragmented and unreal framework diverted from the socioeconomic setup in which they exist.

The aim of this article is to highlight different aspects of environmental problems, the difficulties in assessing them and to understand how evolution of a long-term policy for the betterment of community and habitat can be achieved in future.

Economic Development and Ecological Degradation

The Indian civilization is characterized by its sensitivity towards the natural ecosystem and the indigenous communities were always sensitive to the limits to which the natural resources could be utilized. With the establishment of British rule in India a major change in the concept of utilization of natural resources took place. The ever-increasing resource demands of England were largely met from colonies like India. For the sake of economic growth there was continuous exploitation and exhaustion of natural resources. This led Mahatma Gandhi to seek an alternate mode or economic development for India then he wrote:

"God forbid that India should ever take to industrialism after the manner of the west. The economic imperialism of a single tiny island kingdom (England) is today keeping the world in chains. If an entire nation of 300 million took to similar economic exploitation it would strip the world bare like locust"

It is most unfortunate that there was nobody to pay attention to Gandhiji's advance warning. India chose the resource insensitive and classical model of development as formulated by the Britishers. This intensity of economic growth in independent India has progressed as predatory exploitation of natural resources. An identical view has been raised by Jayanta Bandyopadhyay (1988), who wrote that "the resource demand of development has led to the narrowing down of natural resource base for the survival of the economically poor and powerless, either by direct transfer of resource away from basic need or by destruction of the essential ecological process that ensure renewability of the life supporting natural resources".

One can site endless examples of such exploitations and ecologically irresponsible resource hunger of the process of growth. Exploitation of mineral resources, the open cast mining in sensitive watersheds of Himalayas, Western Ghats and Central India have cause massive environmental damages. Limestone quarrying in Doon valley, Almora and Pithoragarh, and bauxite mining (by BALCO) caused ecological havoc in the Gandhamardan Hills of Orissa. The situation is same in large parts of Orissa, South Bihar, and Madhya Pradesh where rich mineral and coal deposits are being exploited pushing thousands of indigenous people to deprivation and destruction. Large river valley projects cause large-scale submersion of forests and agricultural lands and take a heavy toll of these forests. Widespread water logging, Stalinization and resulting desertification have been identified in the command areas of projects like Tawa, Kosi, Gandak, Tungabhadra, Malaprabha, Ghatprabha etc.

The present development programme is based on classical model of economic development resting on resource intensive technologies that lead to resource exploitation, exhaustion and alienation. Ecological degradation and economic deprivation have resulted in environmental conflicts. Environmental conflicts are sharpest when a project threatens the livelihood of local people (Menon, 1998).

Large river valley projects including the latest controversial Narmada Valley Project has caused large-scale submersion of forests and agricultural lands. Large-scale destabilization & submersion of land by seepage, widespread water logging, Stalinization and resulting desertification in the command area of many dams have been recorded (Jain, 1988). According to Centre of Science and Environment (CSE, 1986):

Between 100 million to 150 million hectares of India's land area is rapidly turning barren and 1 million hectares of croplands and grazing lands are badly affected. Official figures claim current afforestation rates of about 1.5 million hectares. But real afforestation may not even be third of that.

- On the average, every hectare loses tones of topsoil a year. Every six months, more topsoil gets washed off than has been used to build all brick houses across the country.
- Fore million hectares have already been swallowed up by ravines. In the famous Chambal Valley more than 10 percent of the villages are completely depopulated.
- Ore than half the national mining comes from 40 contiguous districts of central and eastern India, the tribal heartland of the country. Several million hectares of good crop and forestlands have been destroyed in this tract by mining operations and hundred of villages have been depopulated.
- The green Revolution pulls out more plant nutrients from soil than it puts back. Many areas, like Ludhiana, have started recording high deficiencies of plant micronutrients in its soil.
- Seventy percent of all available water in India is polluted. In many places the ground water table is going down.
- Between quarters to a half of the lands brought

under irrigation can go out of cultivation permanently because of soil salinity and water logging.

- The flood-prone area has doubled over the last ten years from 20 million to 40 million hectares. And million people have been displaced and uprooted. The country report of the 4th World Conference on Women in Beijing in 1995, published by Govt. of India, HRD, has revealed that:
- Deprivation of traditional means of livelihood is most often the result of environmental degradation, resulting from such natural and manmade disasters as droughts, floods, hurricanes, erosions, desertification and inappro-priate land use. Such conditions have already pushed great number of poor into marginal environment.
- More than 70% of the Indian population is rural based. Development imperatives have inevitably led to some destruction of the biomass through deforestation and environmental degradation. Theses affect the landless and the marginal farmers in rural areas, tribal from denuded forest areas, pastoralists from overgrazed communities in coastal fishing areas and migrants in slums and squatter settlements.
- India has a total landmass of 330 million hectares. In the predominantly rain fed, drought prone and high population areas, there is a severe stress on natural resources. Tree cover has been considerably depleted, soil erosion damage has escalated, the water table has gone down and the severity of drought has increased the ecological deterioration of dry lands in the last few decades. Population growth, poverty, rising aspirations and affluence of the middles class has exerted powerful pressures on the ecosystem. The erosion of traditional institutions for managing common property resources and the failure

of new institutions to fill the vacuum has affected the denudation of natural resources.

Sadly, the impoverishment of the poor is accompanied by a simultaneous and systematic erosion of the basic means of their subsistence: the environment, with its life supporting natural resources - land, water and forests, B.B. Vohra, a member of the national environment planning agency, expressed his anguish at the state of India's environment -

> "Wherever one might go in this vast country of ours. Denuded stricken villages, silted lakes and drying wells are to be encountered almost everywhere".

Together with the scheduled castes, scheduled tribes are regarded as the poorest and most vulnerable section of Indian society. Apart from agriculture, an important pursuit of tribal has been forestry and in this they have suffered a great deal on account of massive erosion of the forest resources. There is little understanding of the tribal forest nexus (Dubey, 1987; Moulik, 1987). When you destroy an ecological niche you push people to unsustainable means of survival like illegal fallowing, encroaching on forest and criminalizing them, writes Meena Menon in Hindu Survey of Environment (1999).

Market Economy and Eco-degradation

India has embarked upon a course of restructuring its development policy framework since 1991, pushing the economy into a trajectory different from the import substitution path that has so far been followed. The New Economic Policies (NEP) consist of both stabilizing measures as well as the "Structural Adjustment Programmes" (SAP) under the umbrella of liberalization and greater reliance on market mechanism (Alternative Economic Survey). The last couple of years have been drastic changes in India's economic policy under stabilization and SAP to meet India's severe balance of payment crisis and to propel its economy into quicker growth and global integration. But the harsh nature of NEP package has set off considerable debate touching the vital question as to how the NEP will affect the environment and the living conditions of our citizen. The ideology of present pattern of development is based on linear theory of progress and equates "development with economic growth, economic growth with expansion of market economy, modernity with consumerism and non-market economic with backwardness" (Badhyopadhyay, 1988).

While the NEP promises to propel the country into the new millennium with quicker growth and global integration, some researchers feel that the NEP may lead to increase in employment. The burden may be intensified by inflation. These may eventually lead to jobless growth, curtailment of support systems and adverse impact of the negative fallout. The supporters of the new macroeconomic polices are of the view that SAP will promote the income earning, opportunity of the countrymen in export-oriented industries, expansion of private sector in the core sector, expansion of the service industry, cash crop cultivation, agri-business, finance, banks and insurance sectors. But these improvements in employment can be jeopardized by relative decline in the traditional sectors as they diminish in importance. In addition, there may be reduction in public sector employment. India is also currently going through a period of trade liberalization. This will have immense impact on the lives of its people who have for decades been living under extensive protectionism, with little access to international market. This will definitely have an immense influence on the lives of traditional community of the country. Overall, the economic pressures may compel households to resort to various difficult survival strategies and hardships.

The technological development as caused by market economy differentiates destruction of habitat by economic crisis. It suggests that eco-destruction can be solved by expansion of market economy instead of having separate plans for gradual economical regeneration. The fact is that a market economy has no mechanism to encourage rehabilitation of natural resources that has already been destroyed by market itself. The price of eco-degradation is borne by the inhabitants of the area alone. In other words market economy degrades nature's economy and enhance poverty, repression and dispossession. It is also proposed as a solution to the ecologically induced poverty. According to Barnett:

> "The inexorable process of agriculture, industrialization and internationalization is probably responsible for more hungry people than either cruel wars or unusual whims of nature".

The resource requirements of the industrial activities have taken away from the traditional or have squandered all the natural resources, which form the life supporting system and satisfy their need for survival. The development of the industrial sector is taking place at the cost of the decentralized informal sector. It is this sector, comprising mainly of poor households, which has burnt the thirst of technological displacement. The organized sector displaces far more people than it is able to absorb. The technological progress and economic growth due to expansion of mines and industries force the affluent modern to coexist with the poverty and the backwardness of the tribal community, and while profit of such industrial development is enjoyed by the privileged the peril and misery are shared by the traditional. Till date, the NEP considered natural environment as an exploitable resource and a sink into which the effluents of an affluence can be thrown. In adopting NEP, has our govern-ment been mindful of the fact that the natural environment forms the very basis subsistence economy for the vast majority of Indians?

Impact of Foreign Exchange

With foreign exchanges as the new god, the government is keen on earning it any way, regardless of the environmental consequences. For example, the export on iron ore from Goa has devastated its once lush green forest; granite mining for Japan has laid bare hills in Andhra Pradesh and Tamil Nadu; the leather industry which is

India's fourth largest export earner has polluted vast stretches in Tamil Nadu and the Ganges in U P. yet these are only the early indications of what would happen to India's environment if SAP aim in converting India's economy into an export oriented economy. When the motive for change in an economy becomes short term profit seeking and foreign exchange earning, the neglect of long-term environmental responsibility grows. Large-scale commercialization of fishing and involvement of TATA's in brackish water shrimp farming in Chilka is causing destruction of fragile aquatic and costal ecosystems of the area. Tourism is another way of earning forex. Many areas which were previously restricted to foreigners, like Lahaul-Spiti, Andaman Island is also causing damage to these areas. Sometimes back, Government announces its intentions to lease out entire islands in Lakshadweep, India's famous coral island Union territory, to international hoteliers for developing tourist resorts. Amulaya, K.N. Reddy (1998) has rightly said "Like many doctors who prescribe "miracle drugs" without telling patients about the side effects of these, the developers do not tell people about the side effects of the project".

Privatization and foreign investment:

Free markets tend to produce demand for innovation, because consumers offer decentralized and flexible sources of demand and opportunity. Government, by contrast, tends toward slow and plodding environmental protection enacted through painstaking rulemaking proceedings. This naturally invites the question of whether privatization can allow government to escape its tendency to fall behind the curve of private decisions increasing pollution.

This suggestion will strike those enamored of government solutions as a bad idea. But we already have some environ-mentally beneficial forms of privatization in environmental law. The citizen suit has privatized some enforcement of environ-mental law and thereby increased the vigor of enforcement. Likewise, "right-to-know" requirements have encouraged voluntary private pollution reduction.

We can design more dynamic economic incentives that encourage competition to reduce pollution, much as the free market creates competition to provide better amenities. This requires creation of mechanisms that circumvent the need for repeated government decisions and allow private actions, rather than government decisions, to stimulate reductions in pollution.

The law can apply to polluters either positive economic incentives, such as revenue increases or cost decreases, or negative economic incentives, such as revenue decreases or cost increases. This reveals a possibility that has received too little attention. Negative economic incentives can fund positive economic incentives.

Governments have already employed this strategy. New Zealand addressed the depletion of its fisheries by imposing fees on fishing, a negative economic incentive, and using revenue from these fees to pay some fishermen to retire, a positive economic incentive. This may reduce pressure on the fish if fees are high enough. The California legislature has considered a program, Drive +, that imposes a fee upon consumers purchasing an energy-inefficient or high-pollution vehicle. The proceeds fund a rebate on the purchase of an energy efficient vehicle or low-polluting vehicle. Similarly, New Hampshire officials have proposed an "Industry Average Performance System" that redistributes pollution taxes to the polluting industry in ways that favor lower emissions.

One can build on this principle of having negative economic incentives fund positive economic incentives to craft laws that mimic the free market's dynamic competitive character far better than taxes or subsidies. In a competitive free market, a firm that innovates to reduce its cost or increase its revenues not only increases its profits, it often reduces its competitors' profits. Hence, firms in a very competitive market face strong incentives to innovate and improve. Failing to innovate and improve can threaten their survival. Implementing innovations and improvements can help firms prosper in a competitive market. One might seek to design environmental law to create a similar dynamic.

One could craft, for example, an "environmental competition law" requiring polluters with relatively high pollution levels to pay any costs that competitors incur in realizing lower pollution levels plus a substantial premium, thereby creating a significant incentive to be among the first to eliminate or drastically reduce targeted pollutants. Such a law would simply authorize any polluter to collect costs plus a premium from any competing firm with higher pollution levels. Thus, for example, a power plant that switched fuels to achieve a lower emissions rate per kilowatt-hour than its competitors might collect the cost of the fuel switching from its coal-burning competitor, plus a premium.

An environmental competition law directly attacks a fundamental problem with existing free market incentives: the polluting firm must absorb any cleanup costs. Because the firm does not experience all of the costs of pollution itself-most are externalized and felt by the general public-it rarely pays to clean up. If firms could systematically externalize the costs of cleanup without substantial administrative intervention, just as they externalize the cost of pollution, then even a fairly modest premium might create adequate incentives to control pollution.

This solves another problem as well. The free market system provides no systematic incentive for environmentally superior performance. The environmental competition statute regularly rewards superior environmental performance.

An environmental competition statute would create a private environmental law, with a few public decisions setting up the law, but substantial enforcement by low-polluting businesses against competitors. The law would create a private right of action that allows a business that realizes environmental improvements through investment in pollution-reducing or low-pollution processes, control devices, products, or services to secure reimbursement for expenses, plus some premium from more polluting competitors. Hence, the scheme would create economic incentives for some companies to become enforcers of the law, rather than creating incentives for most companies to resist enforcement. This would effectively privatize enforcement, making it a private activity, rather than a government activity with some public-spirited private support, as in the citizen suit mechanism.

Such a proposal overcomes the fundamental problem with traditional regulation, emissions trading, and pollution taxes. These mechanisms rely on government decisions as the driver for pollution reductions. An environmental competition law makes private initiative, motivated by the prospect of gain and the fear of loss, the driver of environmental improvement, thus replicating free market dynamics. The magnitude of the incentive may depend upon the extent of industry fears about competitors' achievements, rather than only the limited cost government imposes through regulation or pollution taxes.

Whether or not one accepts the value of this particular idea, it should demonstrate the value of taking on the plodding nature of government as a problem to be overcome by reliance on the model provided by the economic dynamics of the free market. Once we move beyond policy prescriptions rooted in efficiency-based analysis, new possibilities emerge.

The emphasis on privatization is accompanying liberalizations; resources, which were once considered for common good and under public control, may eventually come under private corporate control. This sector has shown little respect for the environment let alone the needs of the poor Shekhar Singh of Indian Institute of Public Administration, New Delhi writes, "almost all the consumer items that are being promoted have significant environmental impacts. The encouragement of consumerism, as it is being done in India, is antithetical to the concept of sustainable development.

Another thrust of the SAP is the opening up of the country to foreign investment and goods. Although a limited amount of competition from abroad in specific sectors may be good for our industrial sectors, but the environmental consequences may offset the gains. Transfer of hazardous and dirty industries to the less developed countries, where the awareness for the economic and social costs of pollution are less than the developed countries will become much more possible with the new open door policies (Kothari, 1993).

If the trend in other third world countries is an indicator the positive prospects of NEP may be far outweighed by negative ones. Ur Government is currently luring giant corporations, many of who have horrendous environmental records. The comings of these multinationals are chilling indicators of things to come. At present the government will have to continue to play an important role in harmonizing development and environmental interests. But will the NEP allow this? It is here that on the IMF and World Bank's insistence on increasing government efficiency by cutting spending should be of grave concern. Countries under SAP conditionality will eventually end up minimizing allocation for those social or "soft" sectors, which cannot show immediate monetary returns like-education, health, development and employment generation and environment. Allocation for the prevention and control of pollution have been drastically cut at a time when the policies outlined will increase the pollution problems. Hence, such cuts coupled with increasing privatization of common property resources shows total insensitivity towards the poor mass (40% of our population) whose every existence is tied to the health and availability of biomass and fodder.

Inflationary effect of expenditure on environment protection:

An industrial country spends a substantial proportion of her profit on environment. The investment varies from country to country and according to different kinds of industry, averaging between 0.4 and 2.6% of the national income. About 6% in France and on an average between 0.5% to 40% total investments on environment in other developed countries (Nurnberg, 1985). This constitutes an enormous sum compared to what Indian companies do.

The inflationary effect of all such environmental expenditure has been the subject of much discussion. Among the overall economic aspects of this are its impacts on trade. An increase in the expenditure of EIA and EMP means over all increase in the price of the raw material or finished good. The company never intends to invest even a small fraction from its total profit margin apart from what it is already doing and also the product control regulation can pose hindrance to free competition. Moreover, the lack of governmental support for fighting pollution and land degradation (like financing at reduced rate, advanced depreciations, capital contribution etc.) is also creating protectio-nist pressures. Hence, the overall impact of any such expenditure on environment control measure causes the consumers to pay in the end.

It is, thus, clear the type of growth prevalent in the market oriented Indian subcontinent has a serious impact on the delicate relationship between economy and ecology. Acharya Ramamurthy (1986) has truly said, "Although our country is free, our villages numbering five lakh are but colonies of economic policy." According to Rothman (1972):

> "The private economic rationality of the profit-seeking business enterprises is a murderous providence because it can not guarantee the optimum use of resources for society as a whole. It cannot avoid continually creating situations which cause the pollution of the environment".

Social-economic impacts of environmental crisis:

The quantitative and qualitative industrial success has produced an entire new situation in which we are very rapidly using a certain kind of irreplaceable capital asset, namely nature's tolerance margins. The roots of current environmental crisis are primarily social and economic brought about by the existing technological move of production, based on mechanized or semi-automated process.

If we look at the environmental crisis not just in terms of pollution but also think how to optimize society's interaction with nature, then it is evident that we cannot achieve the latter on the basis of current technological mode of operation.

On the present forest policy Anil Agarwal (1993) has to say that "even Environmentalist, by and large, have an urban orientation and think more of the environment as the protection of beautiful trees and tiger rather than the MEP, i.e., food, fuel, fertilizers and medicinal herbs for survival of the traditional and other forest dwellers."

Associated with deforestation capitalist exploitation has also resulted land alienation, displacement and loose of social identity. The multidimensional problem of environmental refugees aroused by mega-projects should be a concern of all. Ganguli Thukral (1988) has rightly said that "a human notion of the displacement must go beyond cash compensation beyond even land for land, and extend to compensate all opportunity costs of uprooting from habitats, its complex social, religious, cultural and material ways of life".

Thus it is evident that sociological and economic as well as aesthetic and scientific aspects of conservation must be blended successfully into one single scheme to have a long-term effect. Our late Prime Minister Mrs. Indira Gandhi at the 1972 Stockholm Conference expressed an identical view:

> "Higher standard of living must be achieved without alienating people from their heritage and without despoiling nature of its beauty, freshness and purity so essential to our lives".

The president K.R. Narayanan was right in his caution regarding the dangers of blindly following the path of liberali-zation in his republic day speech (26th Jan. 2000) and said that:

> "Economic reforms in India have not alleviated poverty, literacy, malnutrition, unemployment or ensured that people have access to the basic services".

Statistics will bear out the President's concern, after

52 years of independence still 53% of children below 5 years are under weight, 46.5% of adults are illiterate and nearly 40% of the world's poor lives in India. The cumulative effect of this multiple deprivation of the poor is visible in the children, who are claimed to be the apple of the development (Jain, 1988).

- Of the nearly 23 million children who will be born in our country nearly 3 million may be expected to die before they reach the first year, another one million more will drop by the wayside before they complete their childhood.
- Of the remaining 19 million, nearly 9 million will emerge into childhood with impaired physical stamina, low productivity and poor mental ability because of serious under nutrition and ill health during their childhood; another 7 million who will suffer milder forms of malnu-trition may reach adulthood with less striking physical and mental impairment.
- In absolute terms, the number of debilitated people who will be added on to our population each year is likely to rise steadily, if present trends continue unchecked.

The above complexity can be best tackled in the following two ways:

- To abandon the age long schizophrenia by which the environment has been viewed till date and which has led to the plundering of the natural resources and this abuse has caused the local inhabitants to suffer.
- To reshape the policy of the industries organization according to the above attitude, if such a mode is adopted along with revived community management of resources the future will be brighter. If sustained development is the goal of economic policies, then there is much to learn from the many genuine people and government development efforts that are scattered throughout India. For example, in this interlinked and interdependent chain, man, who is

also a component, tries to remove himself foolishly from this interdependence by simplifying and modifying the ecosystem. This disrupts the homeostatic equilibrium. His way of ignoring the problem only creates others and ultimately threatens his own existence.

Numerous examples is quoted to prove this fact:

- If we consume more natural resources and pollute air and water, the cost of restoring it will slow down industrial growth, which is the basis of development.
- If we neglect agriculture and favour industry the importing of foodstuff will consume more foreign currency meant for industrial growth.
- Keeping pace with industrialization if we do not provide enough fund for community education, the people will lack political cohesion and because they will be insufficiently inform will make unrealistic demands. This will strain the fabric of society and endanger the moral of life.

Environment Restoration

ERA in India is in embryonic state and mainly include cleaning of air, water, soil or biological food chains to man, and is principally linked with human activity like, industries, agriculture, mining and irrigation etc. it should also encompass fiscal mechanism by encouraging those activities that cause little or no environmental degradation and also discourage those that cause problems. Thus it is necessary to classify the activities into the following categories (Sairam, 1993).

1. Non-restorative activities necessary for economic growth.
2. Restorative activities necessary for economic growth.
3. Non-restorative activities unnecessary for economic growth.
4. Restorative activities unnecessary for economic growth.

Such a categorization is necessary because this will enable the Government to evolve a suitable policy framework to achieve Economic Development along with Environmental Restoration. Also specific environmental taxes can be charged to achieve the above goal. While formulating the policy package it should be kept in mind that environmental restoration management do not oppose development and but positively uses the forces of competition. A national team comprising of economists, ecologists, engineers, and tax administrations, environmental activities, can achieve a rational approach towards evolution of a sound fiscal and economic policy conducive to the environmental goal. There can be two possible actions for environmental restoration:

1. Prohibition or regulation of environmental quality standard.
2. Fiscal measures.

Regulatory Policy

It is one of the most widely practiced environmental mea-sures, which control the polluters performance by regulating industrial processes or products by abandoning or limiting the discharge of certain pollutants and/or by restricting certain activities etc. through licensing or setting of minimal national standards, etc. In this case the polluters are left with no other option than to abide by the rules or face penalties. Thus, control policies that impose uniform limitation on all polluters are bound to be in efficient (Kneese & Sihultze, 1975). Therefore, such a regulatory policy becomes static and sub optimal in term of environmental and economic efficiency.

The experience till date shows that very little has been achieved through such regulatory policy (Saraswat, 1987). There are seven reasons why it has failed, according to Sairam (1993):

1. The approach is basically legalistic.
2. As the regulatory system comes into force only after violation has occurred, it is not preventive in nature.
3. Pragmatic waste management through changes in

inputs, processes, by-product recovery, etc. is not induced.

4. It lacks coordination between its measures-shifting the problem from one sub domain of the environment to another.
5. It does not induce internalization of environment protection cost by making depletion unprofitable. Since polluters do not have to pay environmental damage, they do not seek solutions that reduce the cost of environ-mental protection. This affects the type of technological development and works out to be a drag on its speed and innovative strength.
6. The industries do counter these measures by filing cases on procedural aspects resulting in dead locks.
7. It is not the most cost effective policy.

Fiscal Measures

Natural resources are subjected to over exploitation, congestion and degradation, says Dr. M.N. Murty of institute of Economic growth, New Delhi. Government intervention through fiscal instruments, revenue and expenditure, is one of the solutions to arrest such resource use. The tax policy in India is based on the principle of maximizing revenue to meet the public expenditure besides achieving economic, socio-economic and other welfare goals. If the goals can be achieved (even partially) while raising resources themselves, there can be no other better alternative.

The fiscal instrument has not only proved to be effective in achieving the economic goals but also objectives of the govern-ment and act as an important tool with wide impact in environ-mental policy measures. The idea is derived from the idea of Economic Theory of Externalities (Sairam, 1986):

> "Pollution and environmental damages arise from the fact that environmental resources are not priced".

By pricing measures their users (polluters) instead of wasting them taking for granted that they are free, can take appropriate measures to limit consumption and environmental deterioration. Therefore, fiscal measures act as a disincentive to polluters who have only two options:

a. Either pollute and pay; or
b. Invest in pollution control to avoid paying.

Thus it will eventually force the polluters to modify their attitude and alter their behaviour from pollution to pollution control. Therefore, fiscal measures taken judiciously will leave polluters free to respond to certain stimuli in a way themselves think most beneficial leading to environmentally more desirable condition.

Polluter Pays Principle (PPP)

This was first enforced in 1972 by Organization for Economic Cooperation (OECD) and was proved to be one of the important tools of environmental policy. It was based on the idea that a polluter should bear the cost of pollution prevention and control measures. Hence, if polluters were made to pay for their eco-sins, it was believed that the process of eco-destruction could be controlled. It was a "non-subsidy" principle. It was adapted in 1974 and declared that member countries of OECD should not assist the polluters in bearing the cost of pollution control by either subsides or tax concession.

But studies in due course prove that more flexibility, efficiency and cost-effectiveness should be incorporate to make PPP more effective. To achieve this certain economic instruments have to be adopted like charges, subsidies, deposit refund systems, market creation and financial enforcement incentives etc.

India's Fiscal Policy

The Indian Environmental policy is largely based on direct regulatory approach, which is usually too rigid and static and is also difficult to implement and finance. In recent years confronted with serious environmental damages, conventional taxes policy is being increasingly questioned. Environmentalists often say the conventional fiscal structure can only delay the coming up of eco-friendly technologies.

But this does not mean that economic approach towards environmental goal has been totally ignored, although there are no other direct fiscal interventions. There are several other provisions under direct and indirect tax laws of Central Govern-ment keeping in mind the environmental goal. Landmark legislation towards this direction was the Water Cess Act in 1977 (Garg & Tiwana 1987).

It is now time that population control measures are activated in a more efficient and cost effective manner and also devising an efficient instrument of pollution control, so as to minimize the cost of achieving any given set of goals. Otherwise, an unnecessary reduction in living standards will be forced upon the public who can ill afford to bear it. The precedence of environmental accords signed by the governments of the India should be established in the negotiations around, and agreements on, investment and trade. Environment and sustainability should not be limited to a single area of economic-financial accords, but rather be addressed as an overarching dimension and perspective throughout any such agreements. Quality of development should be a key priority. Governments should establish social and environmental limits to growth on the basis of environmental sustainability and social equity.

International trade agreements and nation states should establish plans to gradually internalize environmental and social costs arising from unsustainable production and consumption. If this leads to higher prices, governments should conduct awareness-raising campaigns to encourage high-income consumers to purchase goods produced in a Sustainable way. The environmental costs of transition to trade and investment practices that are fair and different responsibilities for achieving common goals. Governments should recognize that there is an existing ecological debt among nations. This has resulted from richer nations occupying an "exaggerated environmental space," meaning that they utilize and exploit a share of the world's natural resources that is disproportionate to their population and territory. Governments should establish strict timelines to end international trading of products that harm the environment. During the transition period, tariffs should be imposed to discourage trade in such products and prevent their use. Environmental regulations should be governed by the precau-tionary principle (i.e., the principle that, when in doubt, we should take the most environmentally cautious course of action), rather than risk assessment (which applies economic cost-benefit analysis to environmental resources).

Trade should be accompanied by incentives for the conservation of soil and natural resources and to reduce and move towards the elimination of chemicals that damage the environment. It should encourage sustainable development and production close to the place/site of consumption. Social and ecological dumping should be rejected. Trade liberalization must not hinder countries' capacity to channel foreign investment toward those sectors in which sustainable development can be strengthened. Trade and investment liberalization must not hinder the regulation and control of companies and investors to ensure compliance with a country's sustainable development objectives. Foreign companies and investors should be held to the highest environmental standards, and obliged to share technologies that preserve the environment and create jobs. Countries should maintain their sovereignty over the right to restrict investment that aggravates social or environmental problems and their disproportionate impact on the most vulner-able sectors of society, such as women and indigenous peoples.

Conclusion

Whatever the yardstick used for measuring development, if the environment is being degraded significantly, and the degradation is not accounted for, then development will be wrongly measured says Selah- El-Sarafy, Prof. of Economics, Egypt. Conservation of the natural environment should be a national goal but it does not need the medium of national accounts for realizing it.

Natural assts can be conserved by regulation either directly or through policy action such as taxation or both.

No body can deny that degrading environment erodes the very basis of economic development and that the poor often buy short-term survival at the price of longer-term sustainability. Such attitude reduces growth and development. A major task can be achieved if the accounts are made to reveal this behavior. Proper environmental accounting will not solely solve the ongoing environmental problems, but will expose them, especially those that are necessary for sustainable development and for sustainable development and for sustaining economic activity. They will also help in taking counter actions, which are to be perused act vely in order to translate the lessons learned into appropriate actions, and help formulate future policies that would ensure the sustainability of development. Environmental concerns are inevitable in infrastructure projects but with an integrated approach the conflicts can be minimized said Amulaya K.N. Reddy, President of the International Energy Institute, Bangalore. Government must present in Parliament, an annual natural resource budget, which allocates natural resources like water, forests, land and clean air for different uses including the environmental ones, says Shekhar Singh of Indian Institute of Public Administration.

□□□

Index

A
Abiotic Factor, 81
Action Plan, 69
Air Pollution, 175, 183
Air Pollution Act in India, 184
Albizzia, 43
Alfred, 82
American Forester, 21
Arabian Sea, 63
Ocean, 183
Aranyakas, 20
Ahoka, 56
Ashrams, 20
Asian Region, 175
Atkinson, 18

B
Bamboo, 42
Bhagirathi-Ganga System, 98
Bhattacharya, 1
Biological Diversity Act, 66
Biomass of Insects, 124
Biota, 9
Bombay Municipal Corporation, 183
Bombay Gas Company, 189

C
Carson, Rachel L., 182
Central Zoo Authority, 59
water, 182
Chyum Wall, 85
Clean Development Mechanism, 176
Climate Convention, 166, 172
Commoner, Barry, 179
Contracting Party, 145
Customs Act, 66

D
Depositary, 158
Deterministic Process, 11
Diamond, 16, 19
Drought, 168
Dry Alpine Scrup, 28

E
Earthquakes, 37
Education, 193
Ehrlich, 17
Energy Budget, 94
Entmological Divsion of Forest Research Institute Dehradun, 128

Environment in India, 181
Environmental Planning Ministry, 192
Eriksen, 174
Ethnobotanical Studies, 47
European Conservation Year, 52
Extra Oridinary Meeting, 164

F

Fertilizer Corporation of India, 190
Fibre Yielding Plant, 48
Fifth Five Year Plan, 182
Fifth Annual Report of the Council on Environmental Quality, 195
Financial Mechanism, 148
Forest Conservation, 39
  Survey of India, 39
Future Perception of Biodiversity, 164

G

Gachathi, 174
Gandhi, Indira, 56
Gandhi, Rajiv, 56
Gangotri Glacier, 37
G.B. Plant Himalayan Research Institute, 116
Gee, 55
Genetic Diversity, 3
Global Environment Facility, 160, 170, 175
  Biodiversity Challenge, 165
  Environmental Problem, 171
Great Britain, 8
Gurukul Kangri University Campus, 117

H

Hamilton, 99
Hawaiin Honeycreeper, 19
Heckal, Jacob, 100
Himalaya, 26, 37
  Hymenopetra, 86

I

Indian Parliament, 66
  Himalaya Region, 75
Industrial Economy, 16
  Pollution Control, 189
Intergovernmental Panel on Climate Change, 166, 171
International Union for Conservation of Natural Resources, 13
International Biological Programme, 52
International Atomic Energy Agency, 151
International Bank, 160
International Day for Biological Diversity, 165
Island of Cacophony, 187

J

Jamankhata Forest Block of the Sanctuary, 116
Jhingaram, 35
Jhum Cultivator, 35
Jurisdictional Scope, 135

K

Kaziranga National Park, 62
Khoshoo, 2
Kour, 2

L

Lanly, 8
La Selva Forest Reserve, 7
Laurance, 12
Life-supporting System, 196

M

Mani, 82
May, 6, 11
Moist Alpine Scrub, 28
Motichur Block of Sanctuary, 115
  Forest Range, 118

N

Nanda Devi Biosphere Reserve, 76, 78, 84, 91, 95
National Commission on Agriculture, 40
National Wild-life Action Plan, 56
National Forest Policy, 57
National Physical Laboratory, 186
Noise Pollution, 186
Noise Pollution Act, 187
Norton, 10
Nutrition, 31

O

Oats, 48
Olea Cupisdata, 26

P

Physico Chemical Parameters of Soil, 82
Power Commission, 182
Project Tiger, 58
Protocol, Kyoto, 170

Q

Quercus (Oaks), 26

R

Rajaji National Park, 114, 118, 129
Raven, 15
Red Data Book, 52
Reservation, 160
Right to Vote, 157
River Valley Project, 51

S

Satpura Hill, 52
Sehgal, 96
Spurr, 21
Stream Erosion, 38
Subsidiary Body on Scientific, 152
Suspended Particulate Matter, 175
Swamp Forest, 24

T

Tamarix, 42
Tehri Dam, 129
Tourism, 36
Trophic Level Composition of Insects, 93
Tropical Wet Evergreen Forest, 23

U

Union Carbide, 185
United Nations, 134, 195
  Convention on Biological Diversity, 66
  Conference on Environment and Development, 130

Upper Gangetic Plain, 25
Urban Forestry, 43
    Development Institute, 187
Urbanisation, 178

V

Vedic Poetry, 20
Vegetable Fibres, 48

W

Water Pollution, 184
Wester Ghats, 23
Wild-Life Act, 52
    of India, 55
    Institute of India, 60, 64
Wood Smuggler, 31
World Conservation Monitoring Centre, 165
World Bank, 170, 176

X

Xenocatantops Karnyi, 79
Xerophytic Scrub, 28
Xylia, 23

Y

Yajur Veda, 20

Z

Zebras, 3
Zoological Survey of India, 79
Zoos, 57
Zutshi, 98